Into the Heart *of* Mary

Imagining Her Scriptural Stories

Rea McDonnell's book on Mary is just what it should be—one of warmth, restraint, sound theology, and vision. It should be a big success.

Andrew Greeley
Author of *Jesus: A Meditation on His Stories and His Relationships with Women*

Sister Rea's personal love of Mary and her intimate knowledge of scripture have created fresh perspectives on the Marian stories and their relationship to us and our world. Her skills as an adult educator and spiritual director shape Ignatian-style meditations which invite the reader to personally enter into the stories, to contemplate, and to pray. A valuable resource for personal or communal study and prayer.

Zeni Fox
Coauthor of *Called and Chosen: Toward a Spirituality for Lay Leaders*

Into the Heart of Mary

Imagining Her Scriptural Stories

Rea McDonnell, S.S.N.D.

ave maria press AmP notre dame, indiana

Scripture translations are by the author.

Founded in 1865, Ave Maria Press is a ministry of the Indiana Province of Holy Cross.

www.avemariapress.com

ISBN-10 1-59471-207-7   ISBN-13 978-1-59471-207-4

Cover and text design by David Scholtes.

Cover image © Malaika Favorite.

Printed and bound in the United States of America.

To all those connected with the

Academy of Our Lady, Chicago,

especially my classmates and teachers,

and my mother, '35.

Contents

Introduction

So often in the gospels, people are filled with wonder at Jesus. The wonder continues today, especially when we have little scriptural information. What were Jesus' childhood years like? How did he develop his capacity to empathize, love, challenge, tell stories, and break down barriers? What did his relationship with Mary and Joseph look like? How did they help form Jesus? The gospels only provide brief glimpses into the lives of the people Jesus was close to, especially his mother Mary.

We do not know the facts of Mary's life. Facts are not the point of the gospels. The point is rather that we come to know Jesus, to absorb the meaning of Jesus, Mary, and his other friends in order to grow closer to God, to nourish our own spiritual lives. The gospels give us just a few narratives that invite us into the heart of the mother of Jesus. These stories fill us with wonder, a wonder that invites us into authentic meditation, prayer, and a "yes" to the love God offers us. We too can be filled with the wonder Luke tells us Mary felt when the angel greeted her. When we encounter Mary in this text, we too can wonder, "what kind of a greeting might this be?"

In this book, we will wonder through the story of Jesus' mother, as we lift up the few gospel texts about

Mary for our contemplation. This is not a usual bible study with "right answers" to be gleaned from the stories of Mary. This is a book for praying, a retreat companion for personal use, or for faith sharing in a family or small group. As the Spirit guides you, I hope you too will wonder, and like Mary, "treasure all these things" in your heart. Meeting Mary again for the first time? I hope so!

MY RELATIONSHIP WITH MARY

Like many people of my pre–Vatican II generation, my devotion to Mary was nurtured by my mother, who always preferred Mary to Jesus. As soon as I was allowed to go out at night, I began to go to our parish church on Friday nights to pray the Sorrowful Mother novena. All through eighth grade and high school, I went to church as much to see my friends afterwards as to pray. Even when I attended Friday night Hi Club, dances for teens in the parish hall, I first went to church for the communal devotion to Mary's Seven Sorrows. My own painful young life found consolation in Mary's courage in her sorrows.

In high school, at the Academy of Our Lady, I joined the Sodality, a group dedicated to Mary. My freshman and sophomore years in the Sodality were marked by prayers, charitable works, and camaraderie. When, however, in junior year of high school, the Sodality moderator began to effervesce about the privileges of Mary, I became slightly nauseated. Moreover, I discovered that I was actually jealous of Mary. Young people often wish to climb to great heights. To my mind, if Mary already had the highest place in "heaven," why then should I aspire to anything? I quit Sodality.

After wrestling during my senior year with this jealousy of Mary, and coming—slowly—to realize that to love the Son meant to love the mother, I was ready to join the School Sisters of Notre Dame community, named for "Our Lady." As was the custom in 1960, women religious took a new name to signify a new identity. I asked for the name Maria Crucis (Mary of the Cross), always admiring Mary's courage in suffering. When I was given John Maureen for my new name, the image engraved in my heart still was of Mary and John beneath the cross. The more I was coming to know her Son, the more I was loving Mary.

AN INVITATION TO CONTEMPLATION

In this book I invite you to contemplation. Actually, it is the Spirit who, through the scriptures, invites us all to contemplate. Contemplation has many meanings. It is a way of praying, a way of being, to which all people are called.

As a young sister, I stumbled through a particular kind of contemplation, one that emphasized emptying

the mind of all images and concepts so as to be free to
come into God's presence. I felt like a failure. Later
in life, I learned of a different kind of contemplation,
known as Ignatian.

St. Ignatius of Loyola, the mystic who founded the
Jesuit order, noted that at its heart, contemplation is
meant to take us out of ourselves and place us with
Jesus. To join Jesus in a union of love is the goal of contemplation, and the way to that union could involve
contemplation of another kind. Instead of emptying
ourselves, Ignatius would have us bring our whole
humanity to prayer. In Ignatian contemplation we use
the gospels, the five senses, memories, and imagination to grow in relationship with Jesus. In his instruc-
tions on prayer, Ignatius invites pray-ers to enter into
the gospel scenes with senses and imagination, sometimes as an observer, but more often as a participant,
engaged with Jesus in his mission. Praying this way, I
began to contemplate the gospels in color, and with a
soundtrack. Jesus came alive to me.

Ignatian contemplation is biblically based, and
is rooted in imagination. Ignatius asked those who
would move through his Spiritual Exercises to contemplate Jesus as he is portrayed in the gospels. I had
studied scripture formally before learning and prac-
ticing Ignatian contemplation. Unlike my academic
scripture studies, this kind of praying led me to a
fascinating encounter with the living word. Praying

in the Ignatian tradition, I began to see Jesus in a new light. I began to see Mary in a new light as well.

One cannot truly enter into the gospel without encountering Mary. She is the mother of the one whom I came to love so passionately. My passions were waking up in my early thirties. My senses were alive, as John Denver sang to Annie, and I to Jesus: "You fill up my senses!" My imagination was vivid, and now this gift was enhanced by this more than four-hundred-year-old method of contemplation.

As I prepared year after year for Christmas, I did more than set up the crib and put the figurine of Mary in place. Through the gospel passages, I could now enter Mary's life, contemplate her and her feelings, her passion, her faith, her deep devotion to God, her husband, and her baby. And I always continued to treasure "Maria Crucis," Mary standing at the cross.

MARY AND THE MISSION OF UNITY

The School Sisters of Notre Dame (S.S.N.D) prize unity as the deep desire of Jesus' heart. When Vatican II asked religious institutes to recover their "charism," the gift of the Spirit that energizes their congregation, I began to realize that my attraction to these Sisters, even as a teenager, stemmed from the way I saw them living community. Loving one another and us girls, the S.S.N.D.'s at the Academy of Our Lady were living and fostering unity. Claiming our charism, after Vatican II we Sisters were encouraged to join Jesus in "making one," he whose death drew "together in one new family all the scattered children of God" (Jn 11:52). Through Ignatian contemplation, it was a simple step to conclude that Mary too must have shared Jesus' deep desire that all might be one (Jn 17:11). In my thoughts and in prayer, I began to wonder just how Mary lived out this mission of unity in the wake of the resurrection and gift of the Spirit. How did Mary help proclaim Christ's resurrection? How does she continue to do so?

A number of Catholics today may tend to focus on Marian dogmas and apparitions. I must admit that Marian doctrines and apparitions do not interest me. In spiritual direction, however, whenever directees return from a pilgrimage to Guadalupe or a European Marian shrine, usually the site of an apparition of Mary, they report that what strikes them most forcefully is the generosity and hospitality of the townspeople. My own experience of visiting Knock in Ireland, Fatima in Portugal, and Lourdes in France is one of overwhelming unity. In celebrating Mary, the people of God truly become one new family of God. As Jesus drew us all, the scattered children of God, to himself when he was lifted up (Jn 11:52), Mary too has a way of drawing us into that unity for which Jesus prayed.

Mary can help make visible Jesus' dying desire that all may be one, his passion for unity among all Christian denominations. I want to share Mary's mission to all nations, all peoples, every individual and every community that knows and loves Jesus. I write this book so that, through praying with the gospel texts and using your own imagination, you might join in this mission as well. For Mary and Jesus' missions are one and the same: that all creation hear the good news of God's love and faithfulness, and in obeying the Spirit, come together as one community of love.

A WAY TO MEET MARY

Using the scriptures, we will be getting to know Mary as adults. In adult theological education, the teacher must respect that adult students have thoughts, feelings, and experiences of the topic under consideration. After allowing time for reflection on the topic, the teacher first invites a sharing of the students' personal experiences in groups of two or three. Then the teacher gathers some of the experiences of the group, weaving their wisdom and experience into insights from the tradition of scripture, or of church teaching. After the teaching, there is time for personal reflection, questions of clarification, and then a period in which the adult learner ponders: What affirmed my experience? What challenged and stretched it? What attitudes or behaviors of mine do I need to change? What more do I want to know?

This is the method we will use in this book. After lifting out a piece of scripture describing Mary, I first will ask you to *reflect*. That means focusing on your own experience. Reach into your feelings, desires, insights, questions, and experiences, whether you are reflecting alone or in a group. Sometimes I will ask you to *dialogue* with Jesus or Mary, and/or *share* with them or with a group, a friend or spouse, family or community—or at least, in a journal. I will then ask you to *contemplate* in the Ignatian way, entering into the scripture scene with all your senses. If you are more at home with quiet contemplation, be still and wait for the Spirit to bubble up some wisdom as well. Next, I will ask you to *wonder*, to question both the text and real life, especially the life of Mary who, like Jesus, grew in wisdom and grace all her life.

Throughout our absorbing each piece of scripture, I will offer some commentary on the *pericope* (a Greek word meaning a "snippet" of scripture) that you have read and ask you again to reflect. Instead of *you* asking *me* questions for clarification, *I* will ask *you*, and ask you to take sufficient time to reflect on your own responses. This is not a book to be swallowed in one or two sittings, but to be chewed thoughtfully, digested slowly, absorbed for the purpose of coming closer to Mary and Jesus. Finally, I will invite you to pray.

If you are a group or family who wants to work through this book together, you might focus on one evangelist or chapter at a time. Whether meeting every week or once a month, there will be plenty to share, provided each member prayerfully prepares. To end the meeting, the leader or each member might share a prayer from the chapter that best expresses his or her sentiments. Confidentiality is a must, as is respect for everyone's experience. There are no rights or wrongs in faith sharing, and there is to be no correction or discussion; hopefully some people will even think outside the box. If the group is able to be open to all members' experiences, the leader of such a group can be simply a time keeper, moving the members from section to section and signaling when the final prayer is to be offered.

One final note: Chapter 1 provides a necessary overview of Mary as she is portrayed in scripture, as well as some further thoughts on the value of religious imagination. It will not follow the above methodology as precisely as the subsequent chapters will. You will, however, find in chapter 1 material for personal pondering, praying, and sharing in a group. This material will be reflective, dialogic, and prayerful. I will be praying for you as you move through this beholding of our mother, the mother of the One whom we love.

Chapter One

Scripture, Mary, and Religious Imagination

Reflect: What is your experience of scripture? How do you name it? Have you a favorite book among the Jewish scriptures? In the New Testament? When have you felt that a certain teaching of Jesus or story of a healing or a Jewish prophet, psalm, or hero really touched your heart? What did you think about the Bible and God's action in it when you were much younger? How do you think about the Bible now? What is it you really want from scripture?

Share: with a group, a friend, a journal.

In this chapter we will briefly introduce two main themes that weave this book together into a whole. This book does not present these themes separately; every chapter contains a mingling of them. Let this chapter serve as a prayerful preview of the rest of the book.

The first theme is scripture itself, including the methods that scripture scholars of mainline Christian denominations, including Catholic, use to help elucidate the formation of the New Testament. These methods were embraced first by Pope Pius XII in his 1943 encyclical *Divino Afflante Spiritu*, and then by Pope Paul VI when his 1965 Biblical Commission laid out its findings on the formation of the gospels.

The second theme is Mary herself. We want to know Mary more deeply, to love her more deeply. To do so, we will attend to Mary as we can discover her in the very few scripture texts that mention her. Since each New Testament book that mentions Mary does so for different reasons, we will take care not to conflate, or mix together, the gospels which narrate Mary's stories. Instead we will look at her in each gospel separately, and in Acts of the Apostles as well.

Exploring the themes of scripture and Mary, we will enter into a prayerful reading of the texts, respectfully and tentatively hoping to fill in some gaps in what we know about Mary. In this exploration we will use our religious imagination. Imagination is a way to engage scripture, a way to come to know Mary. We want to remember that Mary, like Jesus, is like us in all things. She was attentive to the Spirit; what we learn about her humanity, mission, and ministry, as we listen and pray, will be under the direction of the same Spirit.

EXAMINING SCRIPTURE

Jesus and Mary grew in wisdom and grace throughout their lives. So too the gospels, our chief sources about Mary, also developed in wisdom and grace throughout the first century of Christianity. The material in the gospels, beginning with the core proclamation, which we call the Mystery of Faith—"Christ has died, Christ is risen, Christ will come again"—was expanded throughout the first century as the young community grew, new questions arose, and new cultures were evangelized. The first-hand witnesses to Jesus, his life and his loves, his mission and movement, didn't just remember his words and actions. Long after his ascension, they listened and learned from his Spirit present within them, and especially among them, as a worshipping community.

The four gospels are not biographies of Jesus. They are, instead, a record of the religious experiences of his disciples as they remembered and shared their experiences of Jesus. They were taught continually over several decades by the Spirit. The four gospels are invitations to us by the same Spirit to enter into the actions, passion, and resurrection of Jesus. As *Dei Verbum*, the document on scripture from Vatican II, assures us, although we may find discrepancies among details in the gospels, we can be sure that in them we have the truth that we need for our salvation. The document states:

After the ascension of the Lord, the apostles handed on to their hearers what he [Jesus] had said and done, but with that fuller understanding which they, instructed by the glorious events of Christ and enlightened by the Spirit of truth, now enjoyed. The sacred authors, in writing the four Gospels, selected certain of the many elements which had been handed on, either orally or in written form; others they synthesized or explained with an eye to the situation of the churches. They retained the preaching style, but always in such a fashion that they have told us the authentic truth about Jesus. Whether they relied on their own memory and recollections or on the testimony of those who "from the beginning were eyewitnesses and ministers of the word," their purpose in writing was that we might know the "truth" concerning the things of which we have been informed (see Lk 1:2–4). (*Dei Verbum,* chapter V, # 19)

With overwhelming agreement, scholars from the mainline Christian churches provide evidence that the gospels we hear today were shaped over several decades. They include events and teachings of Jesus, remembered and handed on over time, but they are not meant to convey historical facts. The first disciples passed on orally their experience of the Risen Lord, from community to community. This material, especially the words and actions of Jesus, seen in a new light through resurrection faith, was remembered and used in response to the specific questions and needs of each community. The evangelists too helped to shape the story of Jesus of Nazareth, selecting certain words and deeds of Jesus, omitting others, according to their missionary needs. Eventually the gospels were written down. Through the prayer and discernment of the early church, four written gospels were chosen to center us, the faithful, on Christ, the very center of the gospel.

Scripture was not written to provide us with facts. Rather, it is meant to hand on the witness, the religious experience, of persons and communities of faith. It offers us the truth that we need to be set free and to enjoy God's abundant life now, the truth that we need for our salvation. The word of God is living and active, calling us to use our entire self—not just our mind and our will—to enter into communion with God through scripture.

Reflect: Take some time to absorb how interested God is in your spiritual development, how Jesus continually leads you, how the Spirit continually guides you. How do you want to respond?

Pray: "Lord, I believe. Help my unbelief." Strengthen my faith, please. Deepen my trust in your love and my commitment to you.

MARY OF NAZARETH

As we wonder about Mary in the gospels, we remember that the narratives that include her are not meant to offer what we understand as "biography." All the pericopes of the gospel are meant to lead us to Jesus. When Mary is mentioned, the scant material in the few texts differs considerably. Does this mean that some of these events did not happen? We will never know for certain. It is possible that many of these stories are not facts. We believe that Jesus and Mary are real historical figures, and yet the Spirit does not call us to put our faith in history. Our faith is in a living Word who has introduced us to his mother through the stories of scripture told *in the Spirit*. Each gospel has a particular message about Jesus to give us. Each story about Mary in each gospel is in service of that message.

For example, Mary has a very prominent place in the birth and infancy narratives handed on to us by Luke; less so in Matthew, where Joseph is emphasized more. It is unlikely that either evangelist had a direct interview with her, let alone a camcorder to record her words and actions. It is more likely that their communities wanted to understand more deeply the origins of Jesus; and so the Spirit worked through the evangelists, their communities, their communal memories, and their ongoing religious experience.

We can use our imaginations, as did the authors of the many gospels judged to be apocryphal, gospels not included in our canon of scripture. The first Christians experienced Jesus risen, reflected on all they remembered, and articulated their memories as a clarion call to all readers to choose Jesus and to be with him. We take their articulation—scripture—and reflect on it, using our imaginations as well as our senses, minds, and wills in order to come to a firsthand experience of Jesus risen.

Reflect: What is your past experience of Mary in the gospels? What have you heard when the gospel was proclaimed? What have you read directly from the gospels? How has any of what you know about Mary led you to worship God more deeply?

All the gospels are centered in the work and the message of the crucified and risen Jesus. He is alive and remains active in individual hearts, in communities, in all the people of the world. He is the Christ. Those who believe and endeavor to follow Jesus share in this risen life—now. Because God raised him and filled him with new and risen life, so Mary his mother is just as alive. She joins him in his prayer and his activity for peace and unity in today's world. In fact, much of what we learn about Jesus from the New Testament, we can also apply to Mary. I put forward five statements about her, paralleling her human experience with his. We will return to these statements in chapter 8 of this book. Test them as you read the texts that include Mary, pray, and wonder. Let the Spirit guide you to your own unique discoveries. Do not be afraid of "individual interpretation." You are embedded in the community of faith.

I propose that:

1. Jesus is like us in all things—suffering and tempted—but without sin (Heb 4:15)—and so is Mary.
2. Jesus was growing all his life in wisdom, age, and grace (Lk 2:40, 52)—and so was Mary.
3. Jesus was a suffering servant, obedient, chaste, poor in spirit—and so was Mary.
4. Jesus' mission was to preach the good news and to heal (Lk 4:14–19)—and so was Mary's.
5. Jesus was sent to gather into one new family all the scattered children of God (Jn 11:52)—and so was Mary.

Reflect: Which of the above statements affirms your experience of Mary? Which challenges or stretches your experience of her? What do you want to know about her?

Share: with a group, friend, journal, and/or Mary herself.

Four of those statements above are in the past tense. What about now? The church believes that Mary lives. Just as Jesus lives now as risen Lord, so Mary is alive and active. Hebrews states that Jesus is our pioneer, our leader. He has gone before us in faith and prays continually for us; "He lives to make intercession for us" (Heb 7:25). Whatever we experience in our lives, Jesus has gone through it first, blazing a trail for us. Mary too is a pioneer. She has had the full range of human experience: joy and sorrow, misunderstanding and union of hearts, failure and success, and above all, spiritual growth through, thanks to God's grace, her pondering of everything in her heart.

Like Jesus, she too lives to make intercession for us. Mary is a member of the communion of saints, all of us presently living on earth and all those who have entered into God's glory through death. All our friends and relatives who have died are with Jesus and Mary, in God. They continue to be interested in us, pray for us, want the best for us, and live among us.

Reflect: Pause a moment to remember someone you love who has died. Do you believe that he or she is with God, loving you perfectly now? Picture your loved one in the company of a very human and resurrected Mary.

Contemplate: Take a long, loving look at your dear one sitting with Mary. Sit quietly for a while (even a moment) and then ask to know that person's presence and love. What happens?

Personal Prayer: Is there someone who has died with whom you had unfinished business? Do you believe that person wants to reconcile with you now? Can you speak to that person? Would you like Mary present as a mediator? Speak. Then listen. What happens? Share what happens and how you feel about it with God or Jesus, the Spirit, or Mary. How does God feel? Ask God. Listen.

Communal Prayer: O God, thank you for offering us your Word, made flesh in a woman from Nazareth. Open our minds and hearts to that truth which uniquely is given us that we might know you and the One whom you sent.

RELIGIOUS IMAGINATION

Reflect: What is your experience of your own imagination? How has it been honored and/or dishonored by you and those around you? Reflect on this gift of God to you. Some say they have no imagination. If ever you have offered empathy to someone, if ever you have entered their joy or suffering, entered their world, you were using your imagination. Reflect on how imagination then helps you to love.

Our responses to God's word are unique and multifaceted. God speaks to us continually, and uses every means possible to lead us more closely into the heart of God. For example, in the Jewish scriptures, dreams were a special way in which God communicated to people. Realizing how important memory and imagination were in the formation of the gospels, and affirming that we too are a part of the community of faith, in this book we will call on our own memories of God's grace in our own lives. We will call on our own religious imaginations. Our imaginations are a privileged means for God to speak to us today, and for us to respond to God's word.

Reflect: Earlier, when you looked on and spoke with your loved one who had died, what happened?

If you experienced the presence of that person, it was a real presence. This is God's way of assuring us that love will never cease (1 Cor 13:8) and will reach beyond the grave to continue to envelop us. This is a simple and ordinary religious experience, coming to us through Paul's writing, through our belief in the resurrection of the dead, and through our imagination. Through imagination we can enter more deeply the gospels, enter the word of God to let the Spirit shape and reshape our hearts. As we use our imaginations to contemplate, we will question the gospel texts, and the gospels will question us, all for the purpose of deepening our intimacy with God.

By using our religious imagination throughout this book, we hope to encounter God in the scriptures and to deepen a biblical spirituality. Some of us may be able to quote chapter and verse, but a growing number of Christians are tired of the kind of Bible study that does not touch their lives directly, does not deepen their spiritual life or nourish their union with God. Biblical spirituality means that we engage the scripture for the purpose of engaging God's own self, through the living Word, Jesus. In this book, we will meditate, contemplate, and pray with scripture.

You may or may not be a regular reader of the Bible now. You can trust, however, that God will bring to your attention those things that will help you in developing your relationship with God. Through religious imagination, we will enter the world of the gospels— in other words, we will enter into the word of God. Religious imagination engages all of our being—our minds, our senses, our emotions, our relationships, our dreams, our memories—to encounter the living God. Religious imagination has always been a vehicle through which the Spirit speaks and draws us more deeply into union with God. Ignatius of Loyola and his compatriot Teresa of Avila are only two in our faith tradition who teach us how to tap into this rich resource.

SOME FINAL THOUGHTS ON USING THIS BOOK

All through scripture, God takes the initiative to lure people close, to speak to their hearts. There must be some three thousand characters mentioned in the Bible, and thus there are some three thousand ways to respond to God's initiating grace. Our experience of God comes to us in a special way in community, but it is unique to our own life experience as well. If it were not, it would not be a living word for our lives.

Trust your religious experience. If it is good, it is of God. If it leads you to be less self-absorbed and more focused on God and God's people, it is of God. If your heart is expanding because of this religious experience, it is of God.

Throughout the following pages we will pause to reflect, to pray, and to contemplate the word in the gospels. The word, as seed falling on good ground, will sprout and develop uniquely as each of us responds to the good news about the mother of Jesus. Just as the four gospels were the product of much shared remembering in four different communities, so you will be enriched as you share your experiences throughout this book with a spiritual friend, a spouse, a spiritual director, or a small group. Accepting one's own religious experience may be difficult enough, and sharing it out loud may be even more frightening. Boundaries and ground rules for a small group help create a safe space. Contradicting the statements of others is not allowed, for this is not debate, let alone an argument. Discerning what the Spirit is truly saying is important, yet each one's unique experience in prayer is valuable in building up the faith of the body of Christ.

Be not afraid. You do have imagination, and it is real. If you are able to listen as someone pours out his or her heart to you, your entering their situation and being with them there takes imagination. We are not creating masterpieces of art or poetry, nor imagining an epic à la Tolstoy. We may be gifted with that kind of imagination, but religious imagination is much simpler, more ordinary, and more relationally oriented. Neither will we be reconstructing historical data about Mary nor discussing secret information about the world given through apparitions. Rather, we will be entering Mary's tiny, Roman-occupied Jewish world empathically, so that we can know through her eyes and love Jesus with her. Religious imagination invites us to empathy, and ultimately, to love. As we prepare to wonder through the story of Mary in these pages, using our own religious imaginations to know her, let us pray.

Communal Prayer: Holy Spirit, give us the courage to listen to you and to share with others what you are speaking to our hearts. Enliven our imaginations so we might have a heartfelt knowledge of Jesus and his mother. Help us to use all of our senses, memories, and imaginations to journey toward deeper union with God. In Jesus' name we pray.

Community Sharing: Which is your favorite among the four gospels? What attracts you about it? In this chapter, what attracted you? What puzzled you? What affirmed your experience? What challenged or stretched it? What do you still want to know?

Chapter Two

The Kin-dom of God:
Mary in the Gospel According to Mark

Mark's is believed by most scholars to be the first gospel penned. We can say that Mark created "gospel" as a new literary form. We do not need to be scripture scholars to understand the message of the gospel, but it does help us to avoid misinterpretation if we know something about this literary form, and what the author is trying to accomplish with it.

A gospel is an invitation, and in the case of Mark, an urgent invitation to see Jesus in action, to let him attract us, to throw everything else aside and follow him, even in his weakness, persecution, and death. Mark's gospel moves quickly, events happen "immediately." Through it, we are called directly by Jesus to repent immediately, to believe the good news, and so to enter at once into the action of Christ.

MARY IN THE GOSPEL ACCORDING TO MARK

Mark and his community do not show much interest in Mary. Although she is mentioned in Mark 6:1–6, and is on the scene in Mark 3:21 and 3:31, none of the classic images of Mary come from this gospel. Because there is no infancy narrative in Mark, we meet both mother and son as adults. By the time Mary is first mentioned, Jesus has moved to Capernaum, and Mary presumably has remained in Nazareth. Jesus has begun his public ministry, and is making both a name and enemies for himself. At this point, people from his hometown are saying that Jesus is out of his mind, so Mary and his family come to "take him home"—literally, to seize him. This was a dramatic, potentially violent situation as Jesus' relatives marched toward his house. It may help to focus your mind and imagination if you read these narratives aloud.

First Pericope

Then he [Jesus] went home; and the crowd came together again, so that they could not even eat. When his family heard it, they went out to restrain him, for people were saying, "He has gone out of his mind." . . . Then his mother and brothers came; and standing outside, they sent to him and called him. A crowd was sitting around him; and they said to him, "Your mother and your brothers and sisters are outside, asking for you." And he replied, "Who are my mother and my brothers?" And looking at those who sat around him, he said, "Here are

my mother and my brothers! Whoever does the will of God
is my brother and sister and mother."

Mark 3:19 21, 31 35

Reflect, Wonder: What do you notice in the pericopes from
this chapter? Does anything surprise you? Imagine Jesus in
his own home. Take your time and use your senses. How
does it look, smell? Do you hear anything? How did he come
to leave his home in Nazareth? What might have caused his
family to think he was out of his mind? Let your imagination
roam . . .

Such a crowd had come to Jesus' home in Capernaum to hear him that he and his friends have had no
time to eat, and his family had no way to pass through
the crowd. *"Your mother and your brothers are out here
looking for you,"* Jesus was informed. Looking around
the crowd, he stated: *"Here are my mother and my brothers and my sisters."* Imagine his large gesture of including everyone in this new family.

Contemplate: As we begin this contemplation, again use
your senses. Can you picture the scene, hear the crowd's
murmur, feel them jostle you? What is the weather, how is the
sky at this moment? With whom in the scene do you most
identify? A member of the crowd, a brother, a disciple?

As that person, enter into the scene, into this event, for each
gospel scene is a saving event. How is it saving for a brother, a

disciple, for any hearer who has now been included in a new family? What feelings arise in you as you stay in character?

Then Jesus added to his statement. *"Whoever does the will of God is my brother and sister, and mother"* (Mk 3:35).

Dialogue, Share: Ponder that statement in your heart. Now the crowd melts away and you are alone with Jesus. What do you say? What do you want? How will this meeting be a saving event for you? What does he say to you?

We are so familiar with Luke's story of Mary responding to the angel's request with: *"Be it done to me according to your word."* There, before God's messenger, Mary is presented as ready and willing to "do the will of God," just as Jesus tells the crowd in Mark his true family members must always do. In Mark, however, Mary has not been prepared for the mission of Jesus through the annunciation of his birth by an angel. By coming to take him home, Mary has lent some credence to the rumor in Nazareth that Jesus was out of his mind. Mark tells only of an ordinary peasant woman with a son who has definitively left home; she is simply the biological mother of this carpenter turned preacher. She is not rejected by Jesus, but like everyone else around her, she is invited into a new and divine family, linked to Jesus by bonds deeper than flesh.

The Jesus whom we encounter in Mark has left home and his mother, as all children must do. When Jesus first climbed off her lap and toddled on his own, he was exerting his autonomy, a necessity for human development. When he stamped his two-year-old foot and cried "No!" at the top of his lungs, he was working through that developmental stage elucidated by Erik Erikson, autonomy versus shame. Mary had to let the two-year-old go, take his lumps, run back to her for comfort, but grow ever more separate as an individual. In this scene from Mark, when Jesus was about thirty, his autonomy was more complete. Did Mary think he was out his mind to take no time to eat? Was she worried that he hadn't visited home for so long? Was she alert to the socio-economic-political atmosphere in Galilee, where those who attracted crowds met terrible fates, even crucifixion? We are told even before this scene that Jesus' enemies had begun to plot to destroy him (Mk 3:6).

Before this incident, as Mary prayed through her worries about her adult son, what message might Mary have received? Through her prayer, could she have sensed that God was sending her to confront him about his reputation? The result of her confrontation was earthshaking and boundary breaking. Jesus announced his new family. When the Word proclaims, it comes to be.

Reflect, Dialogue: Now focus on Mary as she hears Jesus say that others are his mother, that those who do the will of God are his mother, members of his new family. What does Mary feel? What does she want? Ask her directly and then keep your mind quiet and listen for a while to what arises in you. The Spirit, fountain of living water, will bubble up from deep within you, within your imagination. Try not to censor whatever arises from your depths.

How might Mary have grown in wisdom and in grace through this encounter with her adult son? How is she like many parents today in troubled relationships with their adult children? What might she wonder? Ask her. Listen.

Where did Mark find this piece of narrative, repeated but treated less harshly in Matthew and Luke? What might Mary have known of God's desires, God's will? Women were not required to attend synagogue and were forbidden to touch the scroll of the Torah, God's self-expression, the "will" of God. "Better the Torah fall into the fire than into the hand of a woman," the rabbis of Jesus' time taught. Perhaps illiterate, Mary would have known, through listening in her Jewish community, that God wills our peace, not disaster (Jer 29:11). God requires *"only this: to act justly, to love tenderly, to walk humbly with God"* (Mi 6:8).

Wonder, Dialogue: How might Mary, just a peasant woman from a small town, have acted justly? Loved tenderly? Walked humbly with God? What might Mary have taught the boy Jesus about justice, love, and humility? When Jesus actually began to preach his understanding of the God of Israel, why might it have concerned her and her family? Ask her. Listen as the Spirit bubbles up from deep within you.

Pray: Thank you, Mary, for your understanding of how hard it is to let our loved ones go. Thank you, Jesus, for setting your heart on the kin-dom, the new family of God. Thank you, God, for this incident which shows us how Mary and Jesus are like us in all things, even in strained relationships. We ask you to comfort and strengthen all parents of adult children who are choosing lifestyles of death. We ask you to strengthen all parents who are afraid to bless their children's attempts fully to embrace the gospel because of fears about status or financial security. We ask you to encourage all adult children who are caring for their elderly parents. Heal these most significant relationships. Bring unity and peace to all families, we ask in the power of the Holy Spirit.

It is highly unlikely that Jesus rejected his biological family. Indeed, while asserting his autonomy from natural bonds, Jesus in Mark might well have meant to include his mother among the new family he was creating. He put the kin-dom, the new family, first.

Jesus' biological family is again mentioned in Mark 6:1–6, when Jesus returns to Nazareth and preaches in his home synagogue.

Second Pericope

[Jesus] came to his hometown. . . . On the Sabbath he began to teach in the synagogue and many who heard him were astounded. They said, "Where did this man get all this? What is this wisdom that has been given to him? What deeds of power are being done by his hands? Is not this the carpenter, the son of Mary and brother of James and Joses and Judas and Simon, and are not his sisters here with us?" And they took offense at him.

Mark 6:1–3

Wonder: Where is Mary's husband, Joseph? He is never mentioned in Mark's gospel. What have you ever imagined about him and his role in Mary's life? In Jesus' life? Ask the Spirit to work through your imagination now so that this man, so close to the boy and his mother, becomes a real person, alive now with God, and interested in you.

So much ink has been spilled to ascertain whether Mary had other children, or whether the generic term for relatives is used for brothers and sisters, that we can easily forget what this experience of her neighbors taking "offense at him" must have been like for a mother. Bad enough that the townspeople once thought he was out of his mind (Mk 3:21, 31). Now he comes closer to them, enters their synagogue. They must admit that Jesus does have a kind of wisdom. But where did he get it? Who does he think he is? What must Mary have been feeling as she heard about Jesus' preaching? Or, did she attend synagogue that sabbath, although she would have had to sit in the back, to hear him for herself?

Contemplate, Dialogue: Enter the synagogue with her, and listen to her son. What do you hear Jesus saying? Listen.

Did she wonder where he got this wisdom? What does she say to you on the way out? Will Jesus visit home after such disappointment with his old friends and his mother's current neighbors? *"He was amazed at their unbelief."*

Picture such a scene: Jesus comes home, and enter that home yourself, as Mary prepares a meal for him. Listen to the clink of crockery, smell the herbs, hear the crackle of the fire. Are you asked to help? Or just to listen? What do mother and son say to one another?

Then he is gone. What do you say to Mary? What does she say to you?

How might Mary have prayed about her experience of that day? Ask her to let you know her prayer. Be still. Listen. What does she say to God? What does God say to her?

Pray: Thank you, Jesus, for creating a new family and including us. Your word does what it says, and so we are your mother, brother, and sister right now. Keep us faithful to God's will in our lives, growing in trust that all works together for good. Help us learn day by day how to be mother to you, how to be sister and brother to each other.

Community Sharing: In this chapter, what attracted you? What puzzled you? What affirmed your experience? What challenged or stretched it? What drew you closer to Mary and Jesus?

Chapter Three

Prophecies, Dreams, and Visions:
Mary in the Gospel According to Matthew

The Gospel of Matthew is heavily influenced by the Jewish scriptures and Jewish culture. Its author, "Matthew," is the authority behind this tradition, although the actual author was not necessarily the apostle himself. The author, the evangelist who put pen to parchment, wrote his gospel both with and for a Jewish-Christian community. So familiar was this community with the Jewish scriptures that Matthew was able to quote and interpret them quite freely. Steeped in a biblical spirituality, the community was able to stretch the meaning of the Jewish texts to tell the story of the man whom they believed to be savior of the Jews.

As living word, scripture has many layers of meaning. Some passages that previous Jewish authors had applied to their own times and events, Matthew and his community applied to Jesus. Immersed in the patriarchal tradition of the Jews, Matthew opens his gospel with the genealogy of Jesus, tracing the ancestry of Joseph, not Mary. The genealogy begins not with Adam but with Abraham, the patriarch of the Jewish people. *"Abraham was the father of Isaac, and Isaac the father of Jacob, and Jacob the father of Judah and his brothers . . . and Jacob the father of Joseph, the husband of Mary, of whom Jesus was born, who is called the Messiah"* (Mt 1:2–16). Writing many years after Jesus' birth, Matthew took an oral tradition that had been passed on for several decades and presented it in the light of Jewish hopes for salvation. That tradition held that Mary had been betrothed to Joseph, that they had not yet "had marital relations," when Mary was found to be pregnant, and that she had become pregnant by the Holy Spirit.

First Pericope

Now the birth of Jesus the Messiah took place in this way. When his mother Mary had been engaged to Joseph, but before they lived together, she was found to be with child by the Holy Spirit. Her husband, Joseph, being a righteous man and unwilling to expose her to public disgrace, planned to dismiss her quietly. But just when he had resolved to do this, an angel of the Lord appeared to him in a dream and said to him, "Joseph, son of David, do not be afraid to take Mary as your wife, for the child conceived in her is from the Holy Spirit. She will bear a son, and you are to name him Jesus, for he will save his people from their sins." All this took place to fulfill what had been spoken by the Lord through the prophet:

> "Look, the virgin will conceive and bear a son,
>
> and they shall name him Emmanuel,"

which means "God is with us." When Joseph awoke from sleep, he did as the angel of the Lord commanded him; he took her as his wife, but had no marital relations with her until she had borne a son; and he named him Jesus.

Matthew 1:18–25

Reflect, Dialogue: What did you notice in this pericope? Does anything surprise you? Reread the passage slowly and pay attention to your feelings. Share your feelings with this young couple.

In Matthew's gospel, the announcement of Jesus' conception was made to Joseph, not to Mary as in Luke's gospel. So much of our artwork portrays Mary responding to the angel's message, but in Jewish culture the male head of the family, Joseph, would be the one to receive the announcement of the coming Messiah.

It is, in fact, possible to imagine Mary, as she is portrayed in Matthew, as knowing nothing about the significance of what was happening in her body. Her menstrual period had stopped. She was pregnant.

Perhaps she was beginning to show. What would have been the procedure for a woman (girls in that day were married at about twelve years of age) found to be pregnant? During the betrothal period of six months, she remained in her own family. Thus Joseph would have known that he was not the father. Whom would Mary tell of her pregnancy? Her mother, who then in great shame and horror, would have told Mary's father? Her father's horror would be compounded by his knowledge of Jewish law. Betrothal was as permanent and sacred a bond as marriage, making Mary's pregnancy the outcome of adultery. Adulteresses could be stoned, drowned, or burned to death. How long did this possibility, not only of shame but also of death, obsess Mary, Joseph, and her parents? What was Joseph to do?

Reflect: Like Mary, when have you been unaware of God at work in your life? Been shamed for something not your responsibility? Faced not public execution, but at least ridicule and ostracization? When have you wanted to speed up a decision because anxiety and confusion were overwhelming you?

Dialogue: Ask Mary how she was feeling during this crisis. Be quiet, and listen. What comfort can you offer this young woman? Then share your experiences with her. What comfort does she offer you?

Joseph was a just man, for "righteous" is also translated "just." He could have accused Mary in public of adultery and brought the full force of the Law upon her. Joseph's justice is not eye for eye, not bent on revenge or restoring his honor in a shame-based culture. To be "just" in both the Hebrew and Greek languages means to be holy, so close to the mind and heart of God that Joseph could relativize the Law in favor of passing on the compassion of God to this supposed adulteress. Joseph resolved to divorce her quietly. He would return his young betrothed to her father. In disgrace, she would have had no further chance for marriage. If she had no brothers, when her father died she would have been dependent on other relatives, perhaps many of them her townspeople. Official religion shunned sinners, and so her own extended family would have most likely resented her presence and her needs need as she aged.

Reflect: When have you, like Joseph, felt betrayed, perhaps in a budding relationship? What did you feel, think, do about it? Ask Joseph to share his considerations as he mulled over his decision: whether to obey the Law and put her to death, or to divorce her quietly. Tell him of your thoughts on the subject of Law, justice, revenge, shame. Listen.

Contemplate: Imagine Joseph at work. Enter the scene with all your senses. What do you smell, hear? Then Mary's father comes to the carpenter's shop. Imagine Joseph's hearing from Mary's father of the pregnancy. How does he feel? To whom would he turn? How would he pray? Quiet yourself. Listen to his prayer in this crisis.

In Matthew's gospel, Joseph was told by an angel in a dream to take Mary as his wife, *"for the thing* [literally] *in her is begotten of the Holy Spirit."* Joseph woke and obeyed, but did not "know" her, meaning he did not have sexual relations, *"until she had borne a son; and he named him Jesus"* (Mt 1:18–25). Notice that Joseph both receives the name from the angel and does the naming of the infant.

Pray:

V: The angel of the Lord declared unto you, Joseph:
R: And your wife conceived by the Holy Spirit.

V: Behold the manservant of the Lord:
R: Be it done to me according to your word.

V: The Word was made flesh:
R: And lived in the home you prepared for him.

Hail, Joseph, full of grace!
The Lord is with you.
Blessed are you among all men,
and blessed are the woman and the child whom you loved.
Holy Joseph, kind and just,
pray for us now and at the hour of our death. Amen.

In Matthew's gospel we move directly from Joseph's dream, his decision, and his taking Mary as his wife, to King Herod. There is no journey to Bethlehem, no manger, no shepherds. It seems that the young couple lived in Bethlehem, not far from Jerusalem.

Second Pericope

In the time of King Herod, after Jesus was born in Bethlehem of Judea, wise men from the East came to Jerusalem, asking, "Where is the child who has been born king of the Jews? For we observed his star at its rising, and have come to pay him homage." When King Herod heard this, he was frightened and all Jerusalem with him. Calling together all the chief priests and scribes of the people, he inquired of them where the Messiah was to be born.... Then Herod secretly called for the wise men and learned from them the exact time when the star had appeared, saying "Go and search diligently for the child; and when you have found him, bring me word so that I may also go and pay him homage." When they had heard the king, they set out; and there, ahead of them went the star that they had seen at its rising, until it stopped over the place where the child was. When they saw that the star had stopped, they were overwhelmed with joy. On entering the house, they saw the child with Mary his mother; and they knelt down and paid him homage. Then, opening their treasure chests, they offered him gifts of gold, frankincense, and myrrh. And having been warned in a dream not to return to Herod they left for their own country by another road.

Matthew 2:1–4, 7–12

Reflect: What did you notice in the above passage? Were there any surprises? Did anything strike or touch your heart? When has "seeing" Jesus with his Mother turned you toward another way?

Only Matthew's gospel carries this scene. When wealthy wise men come to Jerusalem, and follow the star to the child, they find him not in a crib but settled with his mother in a home. *"And going into the house they saw the child with Mary his mother"* (Mt 2:11). One of Matthew's purposes in this story may have been to manifest Jesus as savior of all nations. Was there a historical base to this experience? What is the truth we need for our salvation? According to the story, Mary was involved in receiving the foreigners and accepting their gifts. What is the significance of this?

Reflect: What might be the truth in Mary's welcoming strangers that could lead to your salvation? Ponder in your heart, like Mary.

Contemplate: In your imagination, picture the first home of the infant Jesus. What was the furniture, what was the décor? Knock and ask the young couple if you might sit with them for a while to look at their baby. Sit and gaze.

Another knock. Joseph goes to the door and is surprised by three Gentiles whose clothing and bearing seem rich and royal. He invites them in. Mary lifts up the child. What happens next? Let the scene unfold, and pay attention to your feelings.

How long do the Magi stay? Is there a meal? What are you doing? What are you feeling?

They leave. Listen to Mary and Joseph discuss the visit. Perhaps you hold the baby while they talk. How do you feel? What do you want?

Pray: We praise and thank you, our God, that Matthew, so Jewish, included this story of Gentiles coming to adore. Thank you for the truth we need for our salvation: that all are welcome in this house, in your house, in your heart, gracious God! Open our hearts to those who are different from us in religion, nationality, culture, age, status. Continue to deepen our union with all people.

Soon afterward, Joseph has a dream. An angel again appears to Joseph and warns him to *"take the child and his mother and flee into Egypt"* (Mt 2:13).

Third Pericope

Now after they had left, an angel of the Lord appeared to Joseph in a dream and said, "Get up, take the child and his mother and flee to Egypt, and remain there until I tell you; for Herod is about to search for the child, to destroy him. Then Joseph got up, took the child and his mother by night and went to Egypt, and remained there until the death of Herod.

Matthew 2:13–15

Contemplate: Once again, be a guest in the house of the young couple. Picture Joseph asleep, then coming suddenly awake. How does he tell Mary his religious experience? What do they feel? Think? Want? If God's will is peace, how can this tyrant destroy any child, their child? Could they have prayed a psalm of lament (*lamah* in Hebrew means "why?") as they gathered their belongings? Take a long, loving look at this family.

Reflect, Dialogue: When has your life been suddenly disrupted? When have you fled, literally or symbolically, in the night? When have you had, like Mary, to trust the dream or the religious experience of someone whom you love? How are Mary, Joseph, and Jesus like us in their flight from danger? Listen to them speak about their experience of flight and share your own experience with them.

There is no historical evidence of Herod's slaughter of baby boys under the age of two in Bethlehem, although there is ample evidence that he was a cruel tyrant. What is the deeper truth we need here for our salvation? This devout Jewish evangelist, Matthew, shows the parallels between Moses, savior of the Israelites, and Jesus. Both now and later in his public life, Jesus is portrayed in Matthew's gospel as the new Moses. When Pharaoh ordered the killing of Jewish baby boys in Egypt, Moses was rescued by his quick-witted women-folk. In this case, we see Joseph and Mary with their baby boy hurrying off to Egypt without home, work, or provisions. They are refugees.

Even without any historical evidence, this flight into Egypt is no way fiction. It is a story that carries essential truth for our salvation. Narratives are symbols that invite our participation. Like Jesus' own parables, stories can convey truth on many levels, over many centuries, in many languages and cultures. Stories can communicate truth too deep for theological propositions. Stories touch and change the heart. What truth for our day in this gospel story! God is caring for the millions of refugees in our world today. Mary, alive, feels their panic in her deepest self and can identify with the hunger, thirst, weariness, and pain of today's refugees. She knows what it means to be pursued by a marauding army. She knows the horror of parents who helplessly watch as war drives them away from their homes and their children die of starvation or disease. She has been there. She has felt with them their flight, their lack of everything familiar.

Contemplate: With Mary, try to feel with those today who flee from war, from violence in their own homes, from famine. Ask for the grace to feel with her and with refugees, all God's children, today. Take a long look at all the refugees of the world, and ask for the grace of loving them. The next time you see the news or read the newspaper, ask Mary to join you in a long, loving look at those displaced, trafficked, sold into slavery, abused, fleeing in terror. Or maybe, you could ask to join her.

Pray: Open us, Mother of refugees, to all those whose lives are disrupted by violence, war, domestic abuse. Give us the gift of empathizing with them and the means to take at least one small step to eliminate these social evils.

A third time Joseph receives a message in a dream: to "*take the child and his mother and return to the land of Israel.*" But he does not reclaim the house in Bethlehem (if such was historical) because of the cruelty of Herod's successor.

Fourth Pericope

When Herod died, an angel came to Joseph in Egypt and said, "Get up, take the child and his mother, and go to the land of Israel, for those who were seeking the child's life are dead." Then Joseph got up, took the child and his mother, and went to the land of Israel. But when he heard that Archelaus was ruling over Judea in place of his father Herod, he was afraid to go there, and after being warned in a dream, he went on to the district of Galilee. There he made his home in a town called Nazareth.

Matthew 2:19–23

Notice how patriarchal these dream-directives are. Mary is seen as passive, obedient to her husband, as Jewish culture and religion demanded.

Dialogue: Speak directly to Mary about what her life was like in such a passive role. If Joseph is said to be afraid to return to Judea, how was Mary feeling? How did the couple speak together of their feelings and desires? How did they grow in wisdom, grace, and freedom together as they both tried to obey God?

Pray: Help us, God of wisdom and grace, to grow in wisdom and in grace. Help us to trust that you bring joy out of sorrow, new life out of defeat and death. Thank you.

There is only one more reference to Mary in Matthew's gospel, in which the evangelist softens the meeting of Mary with her adult and very popular son during his ministry. Unlike Mark's gospel, there is no indication here that his family was worried about his mental state.

Fifth Pericope

While he was still speaking to the crowds, his mother and his brothers were standing outside, wanting to speak to him. Someone told him, "Look, your mother and brothers are standing outside wanting to speak to you." But to the one who had told him this, Jesus replied, "Who is my mother, and who are my brothers?" And pointing to his disciples, he said, "Here are my mother and my brothers! For whoever does the will of my Father in heaven is my brother and sister and mother."

Matthew 12:46–50

Wonder: Why might Mary have come looking for her son? How might she have felt when others are called his "mother"?

Mary "did" the will of God. She was obedient. As a good Jewish wife, Mary was certainly obedient to her husband. She would have found God's will in and valued the religious experience that led Joseph, through dreams, to protect her and her child. We too can often know the will of God through simply doing our duty, being faithful to our commitments. Mary undoubtedly would have interpreted the disruption of their lives in the Bethlehem home, the terror of fleeing in the night to a strange country, their years of exile, as the will of God that she would "do." She had the serenity and trust to accept those things that she could not change.

Reflect, Dialogue: How do you describe the will of God? How do you come to know it? Did Jesus include Mary in his new family? Ask him, ask her. Listen.

Pray: May God's will be done on earth as it is in heaven! Thank you, Jesus, for calling us to obey God's will, and for including us in your new family.

This is the last we hear of Mary from Matthew. While Mark mentions women looking on the crucifixion, Matthew names them, and Mary the mother of Jesus is not mentioned. *"Many women were also there, looking on from a distance; they had followed Jesus from Galilee and had provided for him. Among them were Mary*

*Magdalene, and Mary the mother of James and Joseph, and
the mother of the sons of Zebedee"* (Mt 27:55–56).

"PROPHECY" IN MATTHEW

To see the truth we need for our salvation that is
found in Matthew's Mary stories, we must understand
how the Jewish-Christian community Matthew wrote
with and for used their own scriptures, the Jewish texts,
especially the prophets. Instead of a specific prediction
of the future, prophecy for the Israelites was God's
current word to console the oppressed and/or to warn
the oppressors of God's people. Jews who lived after
the prophets would apply the words of the prophet or
psalm to their own events and contemporaries. As living Word, the critique and comfort of the Jewish prophets is still applicable to us here and now. For example,
in the Catholic liturgy on the day after Ash Wednesday,
we hear God speak through the prophet Isaiah: *"Is not
this the fast that I choose: to loose the bonds of injustice, to
undo the thongs of the yoke, to let the oppressed go free . . .
to share your bread with the hungry and bring the homeless
poor into your house?"* (Is 58:6–7).

As the early Christians formed the gospels, they
used this Jewish method of applying certain texts to
their times. We apply psalms and certain texts of the
prophets to ourselves and our times, just as Jews and
Jewish Christians did.

For example, after Jesus had lived his life, died, and was raised, the first Christians found sacred texts to bolster their deepest belief: that all God had done with Jesus was well-planned. It was actually God's will. They also used these authoritative texts in order to counter the Jewish belief that anyone who was hung on a tree was cursed by God. For example, Peter on pentecost applies Psalm 16 to Jesus and his resurrection. *"God raised him up, having freed him from death, because it was impossible for him to be held in its power. For David says concerning him '. . . you will not abandon me to Hades or let your Holy One experience corruption . . .'"* (Acts 2:24–27).

David, if indeed he wrote this psalm, did not see Jesus in a crystal ball. Peter was applying the words to his situation. We too still apply various scripture passages to our lives and times. Let us take an example from Matthew, who quoted the prophet Isaiah in order to state something that was already coming to be believed about the mother of Jesus: that she was a virgin. Writing in Greek, Matthew would have found in his Greek translation of the Jewish scriptures that the word for "young girl" in the Hebrew text of Isaiah 7:14 was translated as "virgin" in Greek. *"Therefore the Lord himself will give a sign. Look, the young woman is with child and shall bear a son, and shall name him Emmanuel"*(Is 7:14).

From this word, "young woman" in Hebrew and "virgin" in Greek, Christians of the first century came to believe that Mary's conception of Jesus was virginal. When the Romans destroyed the Temple in 70 CE and the Jews were exiled from Jerusalem, a group of rabbis fled to Jamnia in the north and established an academy to keep studying and handing on the Jewish traditions. They were hostile to the then still-new sect of Judaism, the Way, the Christians. These rabbis taught (around 93 CE) that Jesus was born of a prostitute. Probably to counteract this slander of Mary, early Christians began to develop a doctrine of Mary's virginity, which became over the centuries ever more physical and perpetual.

Greek language and culture was the milieu of many members of the young Christian community. As the Christian missionary movement spread throughout the Mediterranean world, it was influenced by pagan religions and Greek philosophies. Stoicism and other systems of thinking tended to dualism. Flesh was set over and against spirit. Often in a dualistic framework, one side is deemed good, the other bad. Body, flesh, and sex were considered lower elements of being human, while spirit and mind were elevated.

The Jews, however, did not split body and soul. They understood the human person as a whole, an animated body, or an embodied spirit. Virginity, except before marriage of course, had never been a

Jewish value. Of all the characters who people the Jewish scriptures, Jeremiah was the only true celibate (Ezekiel's call to stay unmarried came after his wife had died). John the Baptizer may have been celibate. As a rabbi, however, Paul was supposed to have been married.

In the course of the first and second centuries, influenced by the dualism of some schools of philosophy, Christians began to value virginity as an ascetic virtue. We do not know with certainty that Mary remained a virgin all her life. Many Christians believe so. Was Jesus celibate? Celibacy means being unmarried. Undoubtedly Jesus was chaste, but was he always unmarried? We have no evidence one way or the other. Mary was chaste, but it is clear that she was married. In the conceiving of Jesus, most Christians believe Mary was a virgin so that God could be more than a symbolic Father, but rather the real Father of Jesus. Probably all Christians would agree that Mary's true holiness derives from her faith, her trusting obedience, so much more than physical virginity.

Reflect, Wonder: What helps you love Mary and appreciate her marriage to Joseph more? That is the core question: love. Are you helped to love her because she remained a virgin all her life? If so, share with Mary why that is important to you.

Do you believe that Mary and Joseph continued their marriage by sharing their bodies as well as their hearts? Do you love Mary more if she were a complete partner to her husband, if she bore and reared more children? Do you love Jesus more to think of him as the eldest child in a family?

Or, can you appreciate Mary better if she were gifted with virginity, "a eunuch for the sake of the reign of God," (Mt 19:12) as Jesus pointed to some so gifted in the community? Let her be real to you, and try to stay open to changes in your relationship with her, and in your understanding of her virginity. Ask for this grace of openness.

Too much interest in Mary's physical virginity can shift our focus from the wonderful good news that God is with us in the flesh—in the flesh first of Mary and then in his own limited, mortal flesh. *"The word became flesh and dwelt among us!"* (Jn 1:14). Even more astounding news: the word takes flesh in us today and lives within us and among us.

Communal Prayer: Jesus, Mary, and Joseph, thank you for inviting us into your life, your love, your fears, joys, and sorrows. Deepen the love in all marriages, in all families. Help us to know that God is with us, growing us in wisdom and grace. As we watch you in action, we thank you for modeling for us how we to be more fully human, more fully alive and so give God glory.

Community Sharing: In this chapter, what attracted you? What puzzled you? What affirmed your experience? What challenged or stretched it? What drew you closer to Mary and Jesus?

Chapter Four

The First Disciple:
Mary in the Gospel According to Luke

Most of what we know about Mary from scripture comes from the Gospels of Luke and John. Both evangelists must have wanted the young church to revere Mary for her faithfulness. Both stationed her at strategic junctures in their gospels so she could model faithful discipleship for us.

Some scholars believe that the first two chapters of Luke, called the infancy narratives and laden with Marian material, were later additions to his gospel. They certainly were not notes which Luke took from interviews with Mary. Perhaps these first two chapters may have been added to counteract the very ancient heresy that the Jewish scriptures are worthless to Christian life. Thus, these first chapters of Luke focus on Jerusalem, the Temple, and its rites. They tell of Zechariah's priestly family. They include a song put on Mary's lips that was, in essence, the song of Hannah, mother of the prophet/judge Samuel, who lived twelve centuries before Christ. They demonstrate the centrality of the Temple in the life of the holy family.

They detail the Jewish rituals of circumcision and presentation of the first-born with sacrifice in the Temple. They tell of a family trip to Jerusalem when Jesus was twelve, perhaps for a bar mitzvah. Luke 1–2 portrays two very Jewish families who nurtured two remarkable men, John and Jesus.

After the story of Zechariah's encounter with an angel and Elizabeth's conceiving, Luke introduces us to Mary of Nazareth. She is called *"highly favored one!"*

First Pericope

In the sixth month [since Elizabeth became pregnant with John the Baptist] the angel Gabriel was sent by God to a town in Galilee called Nazareth, to a virgin engaged to a man whose name was Joseph, of the house of David. The virgin's name was Mary. And he came to her and said, "Greetings, favored one! The Lord is with you." But she was much perplexed by his words and pondered what sort of greeting this might be. The angel said to her, "Do not be afraid, Mary, for you have found favor with God. And now you will conceive in your womb and bear a son, and you will name him Jesus. He will be great, and will be called the Son of the Most High, and the Lord God will give him the throne of his ancestor David. He will reign over the house of Jacob forever, and of his kingdom there will be no end."

Mary said to the angel, "How can this be, since I am a virgin?"

The angel said to her, "The Holy Spirit will come upon you, and the power of the Most High will overshadow you; therefore the child to be born will be holy; he will be called Son of God. And now your relative Elizabeth in her old age has also conceived a son, and this is the sixth month for her who was said to be barren. For nothing is impossible with God."

Then Mary said, "Here I am, the servant of the Lord; let it be done to me according to your word." Then the angel departed from her.

Luke 1:26–38

Reflect: What did you notice in this pericope? Were there any surprises for you? When have you received God's messages (for that is what *angelos* means in Greek: "*messenger*") and by what means did you receive them? For example, through scripture, a worship service, a kind word, a correction from a friend, a dream, a "coincidence" that was too important to call coincidence?

Like Zechariah, Mary was troubled and "dialogued in her mind" what this angelic greeting could mean. How long did she puzzle over this? The angel assured her that she need not be afraid, "for you have found favor (*charin*, or "grace") with God." What did that assurance do to her? How did she wrestle with her inner disturbance?

Reflect, Dialogue: How do you dialogue in your mind? Ask the Spirit to be your dialogue partner right now.

The angel explained that Mary would conceive and told her how this child would be named. Mary questioned, and unlike Zechariah, her questions received not a rebuke and a silencing, but an elucidation. *"How can this be since I know not man?"* For the Jews, *knowing* is such an intimate act that the word is used for sexual intercourse. "How can this be without intercourse?" Mary is asking. Mary received a two-fold answer: First, the Holy Spirit will come upon you; and secondly, the power—*dynamis* in Greek—of the most high will overshadow you. The word "overshadow" derives from the Greek word for the tent (or tabernacle) in which Israel carried the ark of the covenant with them in their desert trek to freedom.

For Luke (and for Paul), another name for the Holy Spirit is the power, the *dynamis*, the energy of God at work in the world. This power of God would overshadow Mary. The angel continued: *"This child will be called holy, Son of God."*

Reflect, Dialogue: If you have children, how are they holy, children of God? Express your feelings to God, as Mary might have on this occasion. If you don't have physical children, "who" or "what" are your children, your creations of mind, heart, relationship? How are they holy?

Did Mary need more "proof"? The angel told her that her barren cousin was pregnant, *"for nothing is impossible with God"* (Lk 1:37).

Contemplate: Imagine the next nine months for Mary. Just try to be with her. That final angelic word—"nothing is impossible with God"—may have been ringing in her heart all those months. What particular word of God (a verse, a gospel incident) continues to nourish you, perhaps all your life? Ask the Spirit to help you remember. Listen.

Mary responded to God's messenger, to God's own self: *"Behold, I am the slave* [literally] *of the Lord. May it be done to me according to your word."* Mary, this questioning, thoughtful, dialogic young woman, hardly sounds like a slave. Let the Spirit overshadow me, she agreed; let the power of the Most High enliven my womb.

Pray: Hail Mary, full of grace! The Lord is with you. Let it be done to us, too, according to God's word.

Newly pregnant, Mary went with haste about seventy miles south, to the hills of Judea, to visit her cousin Elizabeth, also with child. When they greeted each other, the older woman was filled with the Holy Spirit, "gave a loud shout," and began to know more than she knew.

Second Pericope

When Elizabeth heard Mary's greeting, the child leapt in her womb. Elizabeth was filled with the Holy Spirit and gave a loud shout: "Blessed are you among women and blessed is the fruit of your womb! How is it that the mother of my Lord should come to me? For as soon as I heard the sound of your greeting the child in my womb leapt for joy. Blessed is she who believed that what was spoken to her by the Lord would come to completion."

Luke 1:41–45

Wonder: "Mother of my Lord." What might the Spirit want you to call Mary? What if Mary should come to you? What would be your response?

Mary responded with a prayer known as the Magnificat, the first word of Mary's hymn in Latin. *"My whole being magnifies the Lord."*

Reflect: To magnify. To make bigger. Imagine a peasant girl making God bigger. How in your life do you mirror God, magnify God? If you are puzzled, ask the Spirit to teach you.

The Magnificat is modeled on the prayer of joy Hannah prayed when she gave birth to Samuel, who would be the last of Israel's judges. No matter whether Mary sang it under the influence of the Spirit or if Luke composed it later, we learn that either Luke or Mary was permeated with the language of the scriptures. Mary continued her exulting in God's goodness, and particularly God's justice toward the lowly remnant of Israel who had remained faithful to God. All her praise was directed to God, whose mercy is abundant, who fills the hungry with good things and sends the rich away empty. As Jesus will later turn the moral values of his co-religionists inside out, challenging their reliance on Law and overturning their notions of sin and righteousness, so did Mary here. God always remembers mercy, she insisted. (Compare 1 Samuel 2:1–8 with Luke 1:46–55).

Luke moves Mary back to Nazareth before the story returns to Elizabeth and John's birth. It seems that instead of waiting for John's birth, Mary only stayed in Judea about three months and then returned to her house. This was no easy journey for a young, unprotected, and pregnant woman. She probably would have traveled with a caravan. What might she have been feeling?

Contemplate: Can you walk with a young pregnant woman along a dusty road? What do you smell? Can you hear the sounds of the donkeys and camels, rich merchants and simple peddlers? What will the two of you talk about? What will the silences feel like? How does it feel to leave the security of Elizabeth's warmth? How does it feel to face the future? How will she and Joseph converse when they are reunited? What does Mary want from her husband-to-be? Ask her. Listen. Seventy miles. What happens when dark falls? What do the two of you talk about in the dark?

Jesus, as both a child and an adult in Luke's gospel, would always be on the road. *In utero,* Jesus made the journey from Galilee to Judea twice. Luke's intention in constructing this second journey, made because of a census decreed by the Roman emperor, was to portray Jesus as poor and homeless. Joseph, betrothed to Mary "who was with child," was ordered to be enrolled in Joseph's city of origin, Bethlehem, town of David.

Pray: You, Lord, who are mighty have done great things for this young woman, and you are doing great things for us. Help us to believe that nothing is impossible with you, and to trust.

Third Pericope

All went to their own towns to be registered. Joseph also went from the town of Nazareth in Galilee to Judea, to the city of David called Bethlehem, because he was descended from the house and family of David. He went to be registered with Mary, to whom he was engaged and who was expecting a child. While they were there, the time came for her to deliver her child. And she gave birth to her firstborn son and wrapped him in bands of cloth and laid him in a manger because there was no place for them in the inn.

Luke 2:3–7

Because there was no place for them in the inn, Mary labored and gave birth somewhere near a manger. We imagine her giving birth in a stable or a cave, but there is no mention of any shelter in Luke's account until *after* the baby is born. To see a woman in labor, or to be in labor, is a violent and dramatic event. Sweat, blood, tears, cries. All of this for how long? Where? A street? An open field? Helped by whom? If Joseph were a shepherd, he would at least have been familiar with birthing. But he wasn't.

Wonder, Contemplate: Imagine the terror and tension in the two young parents as the baby passed through the birth canal. Enter into the scene. Did Joseph reach for the crowning head, mop up the blood, comfort his beloved, or was Mary alone? Imagine Mary's pain and fear. Ask for the grace to feel with her. Can you stay with her? Can you stay silent and just gaze on her?

There have been those throughout the centuries who say that being without "original sin" preserved Mary from the punishment of Eve, who would bear her children in pain. Is Mary a real woman, or a plastic statue? Why would God let her be exempt from terror when her son was obviously in panic-stricken agony in the garden of Gethsemane? Jesus labored in pain and gave birth to the church on Calvary, so why would God let Mary be exempt from labor pains? She is a strong woman, as are all women who willingly go through this experience of fear and physical pain.

Contemplate: Go to Bethlehem in your contemplation of this birthing scene. Are you under the stars or sheltered by some rough dwelling? Do you help, or are you even more frightened than Joseph? Speak to these new parents. What do you want to say? How do they respond to you?

We do know that it was night when Mary gave birth, which only heightened the terror. No florescent lights in a sterile hospital, no midwife, no mother at her side, no former experience to ease her fright. This was her firstborn child.

Pray: Mother, our mother, comfort all mothers, those giving birth, those struggling with their children, those burying their children. Encourage all mothers whose life seems like night, without hope.

Suddenly there was an onrush of shepherds into Mary and Joseph's silent soothing of the infant.

Fourth Pericope

In that region there were shepherds living in the fields, keeping watch over their flock by night. Then an angel of the Lord stood before them, and the glory of the Lord shone around them, and they were terrified. But the angel said to them, "Do not be afraid; for see—I am bringing you good news of great joy for all the people." ... When the angels had left them and gone into heaven, the shepherds said to one another, "Let us go now to Bethlehem and see this thing that has taken place, which the Lord has made known to us." So they went with haste and found Mary and Joseph, and the child lying in the manger. When they saw this, they made known what had been told them about this child; and all who heard it were amazed at what the shepherds told them. But Mary treasured all these words and pondered them in her heart. The shepherds returned, glorifying and praising God for all that they had heard and seen, as it had been told them.

Luke 2:8–20

Shepherds were considered outcasts by the religious authorities, ritually unclean because of their work, for no one could imagine a shepherd not rustling a lost sheep into his own flock. These unwanted guests, poor, outcast, and probably smelly and noisy, arrived. No wealthy wise men as in Matthew's account, but those scorned by religious society hurried to greet the baby lying in a manger and his stunned and weary parents. Mary heard their experience of angels, and *"pondered all these things in her heart."*

Wonder, Contemplate: Enter this scene with empathy. In the pitch dark, hear the clamor coming nearer. Smell the unwashed bodies. How does Joseph react? How is Mary feeling? With whom do you identify? When you are afraid, do you react with defensiveness and anger, as Joseph might have? Do you withdraw, as Mary might have at first? How do you work through your fears of those in our society who are different, who are marginalized? Share your ponderings with Mary and Joseph as the newborn falls back to sleep. Maybe you would like to rock him as you speak about fear with the new parents.

Recall that in Luke's story, Mary and Joseph are from Nazareth—they are far from home. Somehow the family must have eventually found shelter in Bethlehem, because eight days after his birth in Luke's account, Jesus was circumcised and named, most likely by his father.

Pray: Joseph, as once you protected the infant, protect us, the church, his body. Shelter all women and children who are frightened, abused, misused.

Luke next portrays the couple following the Law of Moses forty days later, presenting their firstborn in the Temple and offering a sacrifice of birds, the donation of the poor.

Fifth Pericope

Now there was a man in Jerusalem, whose name was Simeon.

He was righteous and devout, looking for the consolation of

Israel, and the Holy Spirit was upon him.

Luke 2:25

Contrary to much art, nothing in the text indicates that Simeon was either a priest or elderly. He was probably a layman, gifted with prophecy that both comforts and challenges.

It had been revealed to him [Simeon] by the Holy Spirit

that he would not see death before he had seen the Lord's

Messiah. Guided by the Spirit, Simeon came into the temple;

and when the parents brought in the child Jesus, to do for

him what was customary under the law, Simeon took him

in his arms and praised God, saying, "Master, now you are dismissing your servant in peace, according to your word, for my eyes have seen your salvation which you have prepared in the presence of all peoples, a light of revelation to the Gentiles and for glory to your people Israel."

And the child's father and mother were amazed at what was being said about him. Then Simeon blessed them and said to his mother Mary, "This child is destined for the falling and the rising of many in Israel, and to be a sign that will be opposed so that the thoughts of many will be revealed—and a sword will pierce your own soul too."

Luke 2:26–35

The Greek word in the text that is translated as "soul" is *psyche*. Is this why Mary, with her heart, her psyche, split wide open, will be trusted by those who are heartbroken through the ages?

Reflect, Dialogue: To whom have you turned when your heart was breaking? Could you turn to Mary? Try it. Share one of your sorrows with her, and ask if she ever experienced anything like that. Listen.

Luke concludes the Temple scene with the arrival of the eighty-four-year-old Anna, who joined the chorus, and with shepherds and Simeon, told everyone about the baby. Where did Luke get that age for her? It may be important to notice her age if we are to think of Mary growing into old age. *"And when they had performed everything according to the Law of the Lord, they returned to Galilee, to their own city, Nazareth. The child grew and became strong, being filled with wisdom and the grace of God"* (Lk 2:40).

This saying about wisdom and grace in Luke 2:40 is repeated in the last verse of the infancy narratives: *"And Jesus increased in wisdom and age and grace before God and people"* (Lk 2:52). If Jesus grew in wisdom and grace, so did Mary. She was hailed as full of grace by the angel Gabriel, but imagine how much her capacity for grace, God's own life within her, grew in those months of bearing, delivering, and caring for her infant son. She was full of wisdom, as full as a young mother can be, but how much more her capacity for wisdom increased through pondering all things, joys and sorrows, successes and mistakes, in her heart. She would be full of wisdom and grace too at pentecost, with greater capacity, and with more growth in God's life as she aged.

Reflect: And you? How have you been growing in wisdom and grace? What deepens and expands your capacity for God's life within you? When you reflect on your various experiences, how does God's wisdom shape your thinking and feeling? Tell God what you want.

Between the two assertions that Jesus grew in wisdom and grace, Luke paints a scene of Mary and Joseph stricken by painful anxiety. Jesus was lost to them as a twelve-year-old, alone in a strange city.

Sixth Pericope

When the festival was ended and they started to return, the boy Jesus stayed behind in Jerusalem, but his parents did not know it. Assuming that he was in the group of travelers, they went a day's journey. Then they started to look for him among their relatives and friends. When they did not find him, they returned to Jerusalem to search for him. After three days they found him in the Temple, sitting among the teachers, listening to them and asking them questions. And all who heard him were amazed at his understanding and his answers. When his parents saw him they were astonished; and his mother said to him, "Child, why have you treated us like this? Look, your father and I have been searching for you in great anxiety." He said to them, "Why were you searching for me? Did you not know that I must be in my Father's house?" But they did not understand what he said to them. Then he went down with them and came to Nazareth, and was obedient to them. His mother treasured all these things in her heart. And Jesus increased in wisdom and in years and in divine and human favor.

Luke 2:43-52

In his own eyes Jesus was not at all lost, but right where he belonged. When his parents in their acute anxiety found him, listening to the teachers and asking them questions, he made a small protest, but went home with them to Nazareth. Still, Mary and Joseph's *"not understanding the saying which he spoke to them"* (Lk 2:50) and insisting on his returning home may well have saved us all from one more Doctor of the Law! Instead of staying on studying Law and haggling over jots and tittles, Jesus' obedience led him later to attend to the needs of his people.

Reflect, Dialogue: When have you suffered anxiety like Mary's, she who is like us in all things? What or whom did you lose? For how long? Can you remember the feelings? Ask the Spirit to call them to mind so that you can share your feelings with Mary and so grow closer to her.

Mary was a real woman. In Matthew, Mark, and Luke, we see that Mary is one of us, human, like us in all things. In Luke her humanity is more graphic: birthing homeless and on the road, sweating with panic when Jesus stayed behind in Jerusalem, crying tears of joy to be with Joseph and Elizabeth, crying tears of confusion and sadness when listening to Simeon.

Reflect, Dialogue: If you have ever said to God: "Be it done to me according to your will," what has happened to you? Where have the pain, the anxiety, the sharp grief or the dull sadness been in your life? Can you talk over these emotions with Mary? Where have the joy, deep peace, loving relationships, growing in wisdom and grace, drawing closer to God been in your life? These too are God's will. Can you talk over these experiences with Mary? Try it.

The Cross

We might wonder at Mary's absence from the cross in this gospel. If Mary had been historically, factually, at the cross, would it not have been likely that Luke would have placed her there? Since Luke honors her as a faithful and obedient servant in his first two chapters, he would be the one to assure us that she was faithfully following her son to his execution. He does not.

Pray: Mary, thank you for suffering such anxiety, and yet growing in wisdom and grace through it all. Whether you were at the cross at the end does not matter so much as your presence in the lives of all those "crucified" by war, poverty, and hunger in our world today. Tend our suffering brothers and sisters, we beg you. Comfort all parents whose children are lost to them.

MARY AND JESUS' MINISTRY

There are two references in Luke to Mary during Jesus' ministry. In Luke 8:19–21, after the parable about the word of God as seed sown, some sprouting quickly and dying, and some falling on good soil, growing and producing, Mary and Jesus' brothers come to him. However, unlike in Mark, they do not necessarily think Jesus is out of his mind.

Seventh Pericope

Then his mother and brothers came to him, but they could not reach him because of the crowd. And he was told, "Your mother and your brothers are standing outside, wanting to see you." But he said to them, "My mother and my brothers are those who hear the word of God and do it."

Luke 8:19–21

Jesus has just explained the parable of the sower and seed to his disciples, concluding with the meaning of the good soil: *"these are the ones who, when they hear the word, hold it fast in an honest and good heart, and bear fruit with patient endurance."* He then cautions, *"Pay attention to how you listen . . ."* (Lk 8:18). From his first chapter, Luke has portrayed Mary as the listener *par excellence*. "Be it done to me according to your word." She is, as scripture scholar Raymond Brown titles her, the first disciple. A disciple is, literally, one who learns (from the Latin, *discipulus/a)*. Luke shows Mary not only listening but also pondering, treasuring, thinking through everything in her heart. She, the good soil in which the Word could grow, also has held the word of God "fast in an honest and good heart."

Pray: Open our hearts to receive your word, Jesus. Make us fertile soil, bearing fruit. Keep expanding our hearts in love, we pray.

Eighth Pericope

A woman in the crowd lifted her voice and said to him, "Blessed is the womb that bore you and the breasts that you sucked." But he said, "Blessed rather are those who hear the word of God and keep it."

Luke 11:27–28

What a marvel that a woman would be seen in public in that milieu, and that she would dare to speak in public to a man—both taboos taught by her religious leaders. Jesus, however, broke that "law" again and again, speaking with and listening to women.

One wonders how he learned to relate so freely, easily, mutually, and sensitively with women—and what part his mother played in that ease with women.

Jesus gently challenged this woman, however, as he continues to challenge us today, not to reverence physical motherhood for its own sake any more than physical virginity. Mary has heard and kept the word of God. Luke has again and again painted in story form Mary's usual response to hearing the word of God as keeping, pondering, treasuring the word of God. Whether the word of God came through an angel, or Elizabeth, or outcast shepherds, or Simeon and Anna, or even her son about his Father's business, *"His mother carefully kept all these matters in her heart"* (Lk 2:51). In his infancy narratives Luke has set the stage for Mary as the first true disciple, always learning from God's word and from her own heart-felt pondering of events.

Pray: Mary, wise woman, teach us too to keep all our experiences carefully in our hearts, learning wisdom from our reflection on them and prayer about them. Thank you for your constant willingness to accept the joys and sorrows, whatever life brought you. Thank you for your listening love, and your long, loving gaze on everything.

THE UPPER ROOM AND
THE REFUGE OF SINNERS

In his final chapter of the gospel, Luke may have placed an indirect reference to Mary. It is the scene in which the disciples return from the road to Emmaus and proclaim that they have encountered the risen Lord (Lk 24:33). In that scene, Luke states that the travelers return to Jerusalem and find the eleven and their companions in the upper room. Later, in the Acts of the Apostles, Luke names Mary as one of the companions who was present in the same upper room during the experience of pentecost, when the Holy Spirit descended on the disciples. Let us examine that upper room and its inhabitants on the night of the Resurrection. It may be that what is narrated in Luke 24 included Mary.

Ninth Pericope

"That same hour, they [the disciples who recognized Jesus is the breaking of the bread] *got up and returned to Jerusalem, and they found the eleven and their companions gathered together"* (Lk 24:23). They shared their experience on the road when *"Jesus himself stood in the midst of them."* They all were troubled. Jesus *"opened their minds to understand the scriptures"* (Lk 24:45). In a strangely passive voice, he next told them that *"in his name, repentance leading to forgiveness*

should be proclaimed to all nations. . . . You are witnesses. . . .
Behold, I send the promise of my Father upon you, but you sit
in the city until you are clothed with power [dynamis] *from on*
high" (Lk 24:47–49).

Who are the *"companions gathered together"* on
Easter night? On Easter morning, *"Mary Magdalene,*
Joanna, Mary the mother of James, and the other women"
who saw the empty tomb are named (Lk 24:10). Surely
these women are among the "companions." Was Mary
of Nazareth there as well? Because Luke, in his second
volume, places her in the upper room on Pentecost
(Acts 1:14), Mary was possibly in that upper room on
Easter night. She would have then been among those
whom Jesus commissioned to preach repentance leading to forgiveness. Was Mary missioned to be "refuge
of sinners"? That title of Mary's has provided consolation to believers for two millennia.

Reflect, Dialogue: When you sin, and recognize sin as
sin, where or to whom do you turn? Have you ever come
to Mary to confess, to be listened to without judgment, to
be embraced as a loved sinner? If there is some sin, fault,
weakness, character defect that troubles you, share it with
Mary now. Listen. Then notice how you feel.

"The eleven and their companions gathered together"
(Lk 24:23) are named in Acts of the Apostles, Luke's

second volume: Mary, the women and brothers, the Eleven—120 in all (Acts 1:14–15). After Jesus was taken up, that 120 worshipped in the Temple (Lk 24:52), but they seemed to live in that upper room (Acts 1:13).

Contemplate: See, hear, smell. Join Mary in the upper room as Luke concludes his gospel. When Jesus stands in the midst of the room, watch her. Is she troubled? How does she feel? What is it like for her to hear her son explain the scriptures? What does she make of this mission that they all receive: to proclaim repentance and forgiveness? Ask her how she will obey Jesus' commission. Listen.

Communal Prayer: Mary, thank you for offering us your motherly and unconditional love, especially when we are overcome by sin and guilt. Thank you for being such a faithful disciple, for growing in wisdom and grace. Thank you for continuing your mission, helping us to repent and come again and again to the one who embodies God's mercy, Jesus.

Community Sharing: In this chapter, what attracted you? What puzzled you? What affirmed your experience? What challenged or stretched it?

Chapter Five

"Woman":
Mary in the Gospel According to John

In Mark's brief mention of Mary, we see a real mother fearing for the fate of her son. As Matthew and Luke write about the conception, birth, and infancy of Jesus, Mary's person and work is central, only to fade again in Jesus' public ministry, and especially at the cross. John, like Mark, does not offer us any information about the human origins of Jesus, nor the role of his mother in his childhood. In John's gospel, we first meet Jesus as an adult. While the prologue to the fourth gospel includes the words, the *"Word was made flesh and pitched his tent among us,"* there is no mention of just how he became flesh.

And yet Mary is vitally important to John's gospel. Almost as vividly as in the Bethlehem scene, Mary standing at the foot of the cross in John has sparked religious imagination, music, art, and architecture, as well as deep devotion. This portrayal of the sorrowful mother belongs to the fourth gospel alone. Mary is mentioned twice by John, and never by name; she is addressed by him simply as "woman" in the two

gospel scenes. She was present and active at the beginning of Jesus' work—the wedding at Cana—and
then at the end, on Calvary. As early as in the writings
of St. Irenaeus, around 180 CE, the use of the term
"woman" has led to speculation that for John, Mary is
Woman, the new Eve, mother of all the living. Mary is
the woman who reversed the first sin of disobedience
in the Garden of Eden. In the first episode featuring
the "mother of Jesus," the abundance of wine (180 gallons!) could symbolize the lushness of Eden. In the final episode on Calvary, the tree of Eve's disobedience
would become the life-giving tree of the cross. There,
with *Behold your mother*," Mary would be named the
new mother of all the living.

John's gospel is short on action. Instead, he ex-
plains with long discourses the few "signs" which
Jesus performed. At the first of the signs, Cana, and
at the last sign, the lifting up of Jesus on the cross, the
two meetings between Jesus and Mary are the work of
religious imagination, the inspiration of John and his
community.

Inspiration is the work of the Spirit. In fact, we
say that the whole of scripture is a record of religious
experience, rather than a record of factual history.
All the good news is remembered and recorded by
those who knew the risen Christ, and who perhaps
never knew the historical Jesus. We put our faith in
the living Christ and his Spirit, not in historical fact

or accuracy of details. Let us examine then what the living Christ wants us to know about his mother from John's gospel.

First Pericope

On the third day there was a wedding in Cana of Galilee, and the mother of Jesus was there. Jesus and his disciples had also been invited to the wedding. When the wine gave out, the mother of Jesus said to him, "They have no wine." And Jesus said to her, "Woman, what concern is that to you and to me? My hour has not yet come." His mother said to the servants, "Do whatever he tells you." Now standing there were six stone water jars for the Jewish rites of purification, each holding twenty or thirty gallons. Jesus said to them, "Fill the jars with water." And they filled them to the brim. He said to them, "Now draw some out and take it to the chief steward." So they took it. When the steward tasted the water that had become wine, and did not know where it came from (though the servants who had drawn the water knew), the steward called the bridegroom and said to him, "Everyone serves the good wine first, and the inferior wine after the guests have become drunk. But you have kept the good wine until now." Jesus did this, the first of his signs,

in Cana of Galilee, and revealed his glory, and his disciples
believed in him.

John 2:1–11

Cana of Galilee may have been nine miles north
of Nazareth. Mary was the prime guest, with Jesus
and his disciples also included. The small band had
just returned from the south, John the Baptist's desert
pulpit in Bethany beyond the Jordan. As the wedding
feast progressed, Mary pointed out that "the wine has
failed," or run out. When Jesus asked what it mattered
to either of them, she simply turned to the servants
and said, *"Do whatever he tells you."*

Contemplate: Stop and look in on this scene of merry-
making. Is Mary singing? Dancing? Can you picture that?
How does Mary's singing and dancing make you feel? Watch
Jesus and Mary interact. Then return to the present, to your
very real and daily life. Mary looks directly at you and says to
you: "Do whatever he tells you." How does that feel? Will you
listen to Jesus? What is Jesus telling you to do? Ponder that
in your heart.

Six stone water jars full to the brim became, with
his order to fill them, the best wine at the party. Life in
abundance! The evangelist ends the scene with a note
that this was the first of Jesus' signs which *"manifested
his glory, and his disciples believed in him"* (Jn 2:11). So

must his mother have believed in him, both before and after the wedding. Unlike Mark's placing her outside the crowd gathered at Jesus' home in Capernaum, John mentions that *"after this he went down to Capernaum with his mother, his brothers, and his disciples; and they remained there a few days"* (Jn 2:12). The word "remain" will recur frequently in this gospel. It is often translated "abide" or "dwell" and is indicative of the long-lasting effect of being intimately with Jesus at his invitation. He and his mother remain together.

Contemplate: Picture, listen in, smell (for Capernaum with its fishing industry is on the Sea of Galilee) the house into which Jesus brings his family and friends. Be Mary in this scene that lasts "a few days." What do you see, hear, want? How will you relate with Jesus and how will he be with you? As Mary, look at each of his friends (as parents usually do) and size up their character. Whom do you like? Why? About whom do you have hesitations? Why?

What happens next? You, as Mary, will not appear again in this gospel until the crucifixion. What do you, however, as his mother, want to do? Will you travel with him?

Imagine that experience, and savor it, the daily-ness of it. If you haven't time to read each chapter of John's gospel carefully, scan the pages to remember the events. You, as Mary, are with him. This gospel is inspired, but so are you inspired in this prayer time, this Ignatian contemplation. Even

Jesus' solitary experiences, such as speaking with Nicodemus at night (chapter 3) or the Samaritan woman at the well (chapter 4), now include you at his side, watching, listening, treasuring his nearness. As each event in his ministry occurs, watch, treasure in your heart, speak with him about it. Let this take days, or weeks. Being with Jesus is so much more important than finishing a book!

Pray: Guide us, Mary, to do whatever Jesus tells us. Teach us how to listen so that the Word may continue to take flesh in us. Help us to keep our eyes fixed on Jesus as he moves through his public ministry.

Near the end of John's account of Jesus' passion, the evangelist comments on the activity of the Roman soldiers. In John's gospel, Mary is present.

Second Pericope

When the soldiers had crucified Jesus, they took his clothes and divided them into four parts, one for each soldier. They also took his tunic; now the tunic was seamless, woven in one piece from the top. So they said to one another, "Let us not tear it, but cast lots for it to see who will get it."

John 19:23–24

Contemplate, Dialogue, Pray: Mary watches. Perhaps she was the weaver of that seamless garment. Now she sees greedy hands rolling dice, and bloodied hands reaching to grab possession of her gift to her son. How does she feel? Ask her. Then imagine Mary handing all those children who are trafficked for profit to her risen Son. See the bloodied, greedy hands of the traffickers trying to snatch these children from their mother. Pray for these children, and any who are enslaved, and pray for their persecutors.

John writes of an assembly of witnesses standing by the cross of Jesus. They include two women named Mary. Again, John does not name Jesus' mother except as "his mother."

Third Pericope

When Jesus saw his mother, and the disciple whom he loved standing beside her, he said ["says" in the original Greek, the present tense] to the mother, "Woman, here is your son." Then he said [again, "says" in Greek] to the disciple, "Here is your mother." And from that hour the disciple took her into his own home.

John 19:26–28

Gospels are usually written in the past tense, but here, "Jesus says . . ." The use of the present tense here can remind us that the action of receiving Mary as our own mother is never finished. Begun on Calvary, Jesus is always giving us to his mother to belong to her and God's new family, and giving her to us, his beloved disciples of today. Of course, sometimes we feel so mature that we do not need a mother, but she stands ready if and when we need her. She stands. She cannot fix Jesus. Neither can she control the situation on Calvary, nor in our lives. She silently witnesses his pain and her own heart expands in compassion. With us, with the pain of the world, Mary stands as compassionate witness, and loves. She stands.

Although perhaps one of the most poignant and lovely of all pieces of art is Michelangelo's *Pieta*, there is no mention in John's gospel of Mary's actually receiving the dead body of Christ into her arms. Mary's standing at the cross is John's religious imagination, as he theologizes on the meaning of the cross: *"Jesus died to gather into one new family all the scattered children of God"* (Jn 11:52). We revere this scene. The Spirit continues to inspire the faithful, even though the canon of scripture is closed. Might not the Spirit have infused Michelangelo with an understanding of a deep truth? If so, Mary not only witnessed the dying of Jesus, but also tenderly held his body, as she continues to hold the battered parts of his body, the Church.

Contemplate: Are you willing to join Mary in her own suffering beneath the cross? What can you see, smell, hear as you trudge up the hill of Calvary? Do you speak to Mary, or respect her silence, her way of grieving? During Lent or

Holy Week you might return to this passage from John and spend a full three hours with Mary, asking her to let you feel as she has felt.

Are you willing to join Mary as she continues to suffer because her children around today's world are violated, persecuted, literally thirsting, unjustly treated? Where will your heart take you? To what nation, what peoples? How can you hold the broken body of Christ, the Church?

Imagine Mary as the men anoint the body of Jesus with spices, and bind it with winding burial cloths. Watch her watch them as they lift Jesus into the tomb and roll the stone in front of it. How can you comfort her?

Sometimes we can be with Mary in her terrible loss and grief. Sometimes we need her to be with us in our great loss, our awful grief. This is a mutual and dialogic empathy, one in which you and Mary grow closer through sharing a most significant event. Perhaps you will want to wait for tomorrow for the following exercise.

Reflect, Dialogue: Either it is fresh and raw, or you need the Spirit to remind you of an ancient grief that racked your life. Perhaps you didn't "stand" but collapsed, literally. Perhaps the dull ache persisted. Mary can understand that. Will you talk with her about your sorrow(s)? If you can, do so. Then listen to her response.

Communal Prayer: God, you who are close to the brokenhearted, saving those so crushed in spirit, deepen our union with you through our own heartbreak, and our union with all your children who are crushed. Thank you that Mary is like us in all things, suffering as we do, grieving great loss and her own helplessness. Send her to help those heartbroken and helpless in our world today.

Community Sharing: In this chapter, what attracted you? What puzzled you? What affirmed your experience? What challenged or stretched it? What drew you closer to Mary and Jesus?

Chapter Six

Filled with the Spirit:
Mary in the Acts of the Apostles

Originally, Luke's gospel and his Acts of the Apostles were one continuous document. In Acts 1:1–5, Luke recaps his gospel tradition, noting Jesus' final conversation with the group of apostles. They are to wait for baptism in the Holy Spirit (v. 5), and then they are commissioned. Jesus promises power to carry out the mission.

First Pericope

"You will receive power when the Holy Spirit has come upon you; and you will be my witnesses in Jerusalem, in all Judea and Samaria, and to the ends of the earth." When he had said this, as they were watching, he was lifted up, and a cloud took him out of their sight.

Acts 1:8–9

Where is Mary through all this? Although Luke did not place Mary at the cross, it could well be that in the last chapter of his gospel and now in chapters

1–2 of Acts of the Apostles, she had eventually come to Jerusalem in the final days. She who "lost" her son when he was twelve, then lost him to death, now loses his physical presence in a definitive way at his ascension. Many mothers watch their children go off to college, off to war, off to start a new job or a new family in a new city or country. While they know this separation is necessary both for parent and adult child, it is so often so painful.

Wonder, Dialogue: Picture Mary watching Jesus ascend in the clouds as Luke portrays it. Ask her to share what she is feeling with you. Listen. How do you respond? What deep loss could you share with her? She is so interested in you and all that you experience.

Pray: Pray for us, Mary, and be with us through all our losses and at the hour of our death.

Second Pericope

"They went up to the upper room where they were waiting . . ." [Luke lists the Eleven, and adds:] "All these with one mind were continuing steadfastly in prayer with the women and Mary the mother of Jesus and with his brothers . . . the crowd of about 120 in all."

Acts 1:13–15

Contemplate: Can you picture Mary in the upper room, praying? Set the scene with your senses. Where is Mary sitting or standing? How does she pray? What does she pray? What does she want? Might she use psalms, or pour out her heart to God? Listen to her prayer, or if she is contemplating, watch her face, her body.

After she has finished, you might ask her about her experience of praying, what it means to her, how it is for her.

Pray: Mary, thank you for your prayer then and now. Teach us to pray with your openness to the Spirit, your devotion to God's will. Give us the courage to pray with you: "Be it done to me according to your will," and to trust that God's will is for our peace, peace in our hearts and peace throughout the earth. Thank you.

Third Pericope

"When the day of Pentecost came, they were all together in one place . . ."

Acts 2:1–5

Mary was waiting for the power from on high. When that power rocked the upper room like a mighty wind with flames of fire, the Spirit fell on Mary as well as on the Twelve and the rest of the company. Our artwork often portrays Mary and the Twelve, but there were 120 gathered. "They were all filled with the Holy

Spirit and began to speak in other tongues as the Spirit gave them to speak" (Acts 2:4). The crowd of pilgrims heard "them speaking in [his/her] own language" (Acts 2:5).

All 120 were filled with the Spirit. All would have spoken as the Spirit inspired them. Mary too undoubtedly was speaking in tongues, and was filled with every gift of the Spirit that Peter, James, John, and the others would have received that memorable morning.

Wonder, Reflect: What gifts of the Spirit might Mary have received in this baptism by the Spirit? Remember your own experience of being rocked by the Spirit or of being gently caressed by this power. What gifts did you receive? How were you changed?

Remember, or find in your New Testament, all the gifts of the Spirit that Paul lists in Romans 12, or in 1 Corinthians 12, and the greatest of gifts, love, in 1 Corinthians 13. Which ones might have been given to Mary for the sake of furthering the mission of Jesus? Paul lists the fruits of the Spirit in Galatians 5:22. What might have happened to the "love, peace, joy, kindness, patience, and faithfulness" in which Mary was already growing when this onrush of fruitful power filled her mind and heart? Imagine it. There are no boundaries when the Spirit fills her, or us.

In our society it is a truism that midlife often provides a catalyst for major change. Women who have stayed home suddenly seek a career; men who have been outwardly directed in their work now turn to relationships as central. Let us estimate that Mary was about forty-three years old at pentecost. She was gifted for ministry, she was empowered for mission. What happens next? Luke does not elucidate further.

Reflect, Contemplate: Have you reached midlife yet? If so, around that time of crisis, what changes of attitude, relationship, ambition, work happened to you? What new choices did you make? Ask the Spirit to help you remember. Sit quietly.

If you have not yet reached midlife, what do you think you might want changed or deepened? Tell the Spirit your desires.

And now? What do you deeply desire from God and for God? Sit quietly again, and let the flame of God's love appear not over your head but in your heart. Contemplate the Spirit in your own heart. Let the Spirit inspire you.

Earlier in this chapter we asked Mary to teach us to pray. Here is good news: We cannot fail in prayer. There is no such thing as an unworthy prayer or a poor prayer session because it is the Spirit who prays within us, putting our unutterable groanings into words that God can understand (Rom 8:26).

Dialogue: As Mary left the upper room to face a life without the physical presence of Jesus, what might have been her unutterable groanings? Ask her. Listen.

Now the Spirit is not just overshadowing her but is also filling her. How does she make sense of this paradox: physical absence and fullness of presence? Ask her.

Mary, the first disciple in Luke's theology, learns from Jesus perhaps more deeply now that he is able to live within her. If Paul can say, *"It is no longer I who lives but Christ lives in me"* (Gal 2:20), how much more Mary? What might that experience of ongoing, growing, deepening, and expanding union mean to Mary? Ask her. Listen.

In Luke and Luke alone, Jesus prays for forgiveness on the cross. He does not himself forgive his persecutors but asks, *"Father, forgive them, for they know not what they do."*

Wonder, Reflect: How does Mary learn from the risen Lord how to forgive the murderers of her son? How long does it take? How have you been blessed with the gift of forgiving? How did it happen? How did Mary receive this grace? Is there anyone who needs your forgiving now? Do not grit your teeth and say the words. "We cannot forgive." Forgiveness is God's gift, but let us pray with Mary and Jesus: *"Father, forgive them, for they know not what they do."* Be open to God's giving you the gift of forgiving.

Communal Prayer: Thank you, Mary, that you too are our pioneer, like us in all things, suffering with Jesus, learning obedience, learning in a more mature way to surrender, to hand over everything to God in trust, poor in spirit, needing God's gift to forgive, to gather the outcasts and sinners into the new family your son created. Thank you for your healing ministry, and your mission to all nations of the world.

Community Sharing: In this chapter, what attracted you? What puzzled you? What affirmed your experience? What challenged or stretched it? What drew you closer to Mary, to Jesus?

Chapter Seven

Imagining the Journey:
The Mission, Aging, and Death of Mary

In the early centuries of the Church, authors of apocryphal gospels used their imaginations to wonder about the early life of Mary. They treat her birth, childhood, and betrothal to Joseph. In the same way, we are using our religious imaginations to wonder about Mary. Because we are an aging Church, because our elderly often complain that Jesus did not have to suffer the pain and debilities of old age, let us then, using our imaginations in prayer, wonder about Mary's later life. Let us continue to see how Mary, filled with the pentecost fire of the Spirit, grew not only in wisdom and grace, but in age as well. First, let us wonder through her whole life. Each of these questions might engage you for an entire period of prayer.

Wonder: Ask the Spirit to teach you more about Mary. For example, during Jesus' "hidden life," what was her life like in rearing Jesus? In loving Joseph?

In your contemplation of the holy family, what would their flight into Egypt and their life there have been like?

Back in Nazareth, how would Mary and Joseph have trained Jesus, and what about his schooling? How did they foster his faith? What was their family prayer like? Their family meals? How did they play together? Work together?

What happened to Joseph? If he died, was Jesus with him? How was Mary able to deal with such a loss? Ask her.

Did Jesus discuss with Mary his plans to move away and begin his preaching mission? How did they discern this move? What was she feeling?

Without modern communication, how did she learn of his activities on the road, and what did she feel?

What was Mary's life like those two days between Calvary and the empty tomb?

As Ignatius of Loyola would have us do, imagine the first meeting of Mary with her son raised from the dead. What would they have felt? What might they have said to each other? Be there. Watch them. Listen.

After pentecost, what gifts of the Spirit impelled her? Where, what, how was her mission? How did she serve the community and witness to those interested in her son? How did she pray?

On pentecost, she would have received the same energy and power of the Spirit as the Twelve. She did not return to Nazareth to darn socks! Legend puts her in Ephesus, center of devotion to the great Mother-Goddess of the Greeks. Ephesus was also the supposed home of John the apostle, and a city where Paul spent a great deal of time as a Christian missionary.

Scholars tend to think that Mary stayed in Jerusalem, the birthplace of the first Christian community. If Mary's mission were in Jerusalem, because Jewish men were forbidden to speak to Jewish women outside the family, her outreach would have been to proclaim Jesus as Messiah to other Jewish women. Her ministry, the building up of the young community, would have been to other women believers and to women who were newcomers to the faith.

Reflect: Many people encourage newcomers to baptism or to a particular church. Remember your own ministry of welcoming with good news, or remember those women and men who welcomed you. How did you respond to their service? And now? What do you want? A smile to a stranger on the street can be a blessing, offering them a small and silent welcome to the life of Christ within you.

The Jerusalem community of believers maintained their Jewish religion, according to Acts of the Apostles. They were considered a sect of Judaism and were named the Way, or the Nazarenes, after Jesus' hometown.

First Pericope

All who believed were together and had all things in common; they would sell their possessions and goods and distribute the proceeds to all, as any had need. Day by day, as they spent much time together in the Temple, they broke bread at home and ate their food with glad and generous hearts, praising God and having the good will of the people. And day by day the Lord added to their number those who were being saved.

Acts 2:44–47

Wonder, Contemplate: What might Mary have been doing "day by day" during this time of growth in the new community? Be still and let scenes, sounds, smells come to you as the Spirit brings them to your consciousness. Be still and just feel them.

Pray: How the unity of this first community must have brought joy to your heart, Mary! Help us to grow less selfish as we learn to hold more and more in common, on a local level of course, but especially with the destitute nations of our world.

While Luke paints a fairly peaceful picture of their community life, there were some disputes. One of the first was between the Greek-speaking (but still Jewish)

Christian widows (Hellenists, from the Greek word, *hellene* for "Greek") who felt that they were not receiving their share of the communal goods. The "Hebrew" widows (the more local, Aramaic-speaking Jews) were being favored. Note, both these groups are Christians, and both are originally of the Jewish faith. But the Hellenists and Hebrews, as Luke calls them, were of two different languages and cultures. In response, the apostles decided to appoint seven Greek-speaking men to distribute alms.

Second Pericope

Now during those days, when the disciples were increasing in number, the Hellenists complained against the Hebrews because their widows were being neglected in the daily distribution of food.

Acts 6:1

Wonder, Reflect: Where might Mary have been during this time when some women in the community felt neglected? Where might Mary be today when some women in the Church feel neglected?

How might Mary have contributed to the food supply, to serving tables, to the reconciliation needed between the two groups of women? Let your religious imagination flow in great detail. Enjoy this religious experience.

Not able to speak Greek, how would Mary have communicated with the group that felt neglected and marginalized? How do you, how can you, communicate with those whose language you do not speak? Ask the Spirit both to rouse your memory and to point you to the future.

Pray: Mary, teach us to reverence other cultures, to look for and act for a more just distribution of this world's goods, especially water and food.

If, on the other hand, Mary traveled to Ephesus, what did that missionary journey entail? We know enough from Paul's accounts of shipwreck that she certainly did not board a cruise ship. It was likely a difficult journey.

Wonder, Imagine: Ask Mary to share with you her desires, her fears, her energy, her caution as she prepared to venture into a new country, a new culture, a pagan land. Listen.

She boards the ship. What happens? How does she occupy her time?

She arrives. Who welcomes her? Where does she go to live? To listen, preach, teach, and counsel? To love? See, smell, hear, feel all that she does. Enjoy the details which the Spirit bubbles up from your religious imagination.

Might Mary have influenced Paul during his stays in Ephesus? Trained as a rabbi, Paul (then Saul) would have been imbued with a sense of patriarchal superiority over women, praying each morning in gratitude that God had not created him a Gentile, a slave, or a woman. However, by the time he wrote to the Galatians, he knew that in Christ *"there is no Jew nor Gentile, no slave nor free, no male nor female, for all are one in Christ"* (Gal 3:28). Who helped Paul learn that in Christ all barriers between peoples and classes and genders are dissolved? A woman? Mary?

No matter which city could claim her presence, she was aging with grace and with deepening zeal for the good news that her son embodied. Her passion for everyone to know her son and his mission would have expanded, even as her body diminished. Perhaps her eyes dimmed, and she did not have glasses; her hearing weakened, and there were no hearing aids. She slept on a mat on the floor in all kinds of climate, without central heating or air conditioning. Arthritis could have gnawed at her joints and still she climbed off that mat day after day to move among the people, or to welcome them in her home. She is our pioneer as she grew, not only in wisdom and grace, but also in aging.

Reflect: What joys have come to you with aging? What physical pain? What limits and loss? What does wisdom look like in your life right now? Mary, like us in all things, would have experienced all of that.

Wonder: Perhaps Mary even knew the joy of grandchildren? We wonder. Ask her to share her aging process, its joys and sorrows, with you.

How did she pray as she aged? How did her prayer change? Ask her.

MARY'S DYING

She is like us in all things, experiencing both the limits and, gradually, the peaceful acceptance of the aging process, knowing that she was moving toward death. She was becoming ever more fully human and fully alive in spirit, even as her body was failing.

Wonder: Suppose she were completely an invalid. What might her fears and frustrations have been? What of her mission then? To whom would she minister, and how? How would she pray? Who would care for her? How did she deal with her dependence?

Suppose a heart attack carried her away. What might her last words have been? Ask her. Listen. What do you want your last words to be? Speak them often every day.

Reflect, Share: What do you believe about life after death? What experience do you have that Jesus is alive? That Mary is alive? That your loved ones who have died are really alive in the risen glory of Christ and in the everlasting and dynamic presence of God? How do you feel about that? Share your feelings with Christ, your pioneer through death into life.

Pray: Holy Mary, mother of God, pray for us, now and at the hour of our death.

MARY'S MISSION CONTINUES TODAY

Mary continues her mission today, reaching out to the neglected and outcast in this century. Luke's gospel depicts Mary as prophet. Mary's reception of the angelic message in Nazareth (Lk 1:26–38) has all the marks of a Jewish prophetic commission. Remember that prophecy is not specific prediction. A prophet is so close to the mind and heart of God that the prophet dares to speak in God's name, consoling the afflicted or critiquing the oppressors of God's little ones. Rejoicing in the Holy Spirit, Mary once sang the Magnificat (Lk 1:46–55). Mary speaks both consolation and critique to her people and to ours today. The prophetic proclamation by this Jewish peasant girl was so threatening to the authorities in Guatemala in the 1970s that they forbade the recitation of the Magnificat.

Mary Prays, Mary Sings

My whole being magnifies the Lord,

My spirit rejoices in God, my Savior.

God has looked on the humiliation of a handmaid.

Behold, all generations will call me blessed

because the One who is mighty has done great things for
    me.

Holy is God's name!

God's mercy is from generation to generation on those
    who fear God.

God's arm is mighty.

God has scattered the arrogant in the plans of their hearts,

has pulled down the powerful from their thrones, and

has lifted up the humble ones.

God has filled the hungry with good things

and has sent the rich away, empty.

God has helped Israel to remember mercy,

speaking to our ancestors Abraham, Sarah, and their
    descendants forever.

In her definitive work on Mary, *Truly Our Sister,*
theologian Elizabeth Johnson quotes Third World
theologian R. J. Raja's comment on the Magnificat (p.
269). Raja notes that God will overturn "all satanic
structures of oppression, inhuman establishments of
inequality, and systems which generate slavery . . .
including those that debase people on account of their

birth, caste, sex, creed, color, religion, tenets, weakness, and poverty."

In her song, Mary lists just why the Messiah is necessary, just why, as the Christmas hymn puts it, "the weary world rejoices." As a young wife and mother she lived in a land occupied by a foreign power (to whom her family paid taxes), under the rule of a despotic Herod (to whom her family paid taxes), and a legalistic religious authority (to whom her family paid taxes). She probably had directly felt the arrogance of the powerful and the hunger of her people, for food and for justice.

Wonder: How did Mary's gift of prophecy develop? Whom did she comfort? How did she challenge?

In Mary and in her son, "justice and peace shall kiss, and truth shall spring out of the earth" (Ps 85). Through her, God would endow Jesus not only with genetic makeup and facial features, but with justice. God's anointed (*messiah* in Hebrew; *christos* in Greek) will do justice for the people (Ps 72).

"God's anointed" in Psalm 72 originally refers to King Solomon. Of course, the early Christians applied the psalm to the Messiah, whom they believed to be Jesus. Mary too was anointed by the Spirit. As, in our baptism, are we.

Pray: Take Psalm 72 and, standing with Mary in the communion of saints, pray this promise of justice together. Feel free to change your translation of "Messiah" to "Mary"; in the translation below, the pronoun "he" is changed to "she." Another time, change it to the first person. Apply the scripture to yourself. As you pray, especially be aware of those members of the body of Christ who are imprisoned in grinding poverty or pain, who may be too desperate to pray, and who need our prayer.

Psalm 72

Give Mary your justice, O God, and your righteousness to
   her.

May she judge your people . . . and the poor with justice . . .

May she defend the cause of the poor of the people,

give deliverance to the needy, and crush the oppressor.

May Mary live while the sun endures, as long as the moon . . .

May she be like rain that falls on mown grass,

like showers that water the earth.

In her days may justice flourish and peace till the moon is
   no more.

May she rule from sea to sea . . .

May all nations give her honor.

For she delivers the needy when they call,

The poor and those who have no helper,

She has pity on the weak and the needy and saves their lives . . .

Precious is their blood in her sight.

Long may Mary live! . . .

May her name endure forever, and her fame as long as the sun.

May all nations be blessed in her.

And may God be blessed; may God's glory fill the earth!

We can of course pray any or all the psalms in the company of Mary, wondering how and when she might have used them. For example, were we to pray Psalm 71 with her, referring to her, we might uncover some of her very real feelings which she would have poured out to God, and perhaps still does.

Psalm 71

In you I take refuge, O God; let me never be put to shame . . .

For you, O God, are my hope, my trust from my youth.

Upon you I have leaned from birth.

It was you who took me from my mother's womb.

My praise is continually of you . . .

My mouth is filled with your praise, your glory all day long.

Do not cast me off in the time of old age;

Do not forsake me when my strength is spent . . .

O God, from my youth you have taught me,

And I still proclaim your wondrous deeds.

So even to old age and gray hairs,

O God, do not forsake me . . .

You who have made me see many troubles and calamities
will revive me again . . . .

You will increase my honor, and comfort me once again.

We conclude this chapter about Mary's mission and her aging, yet on fire with the Spirit, with a biblical, contemporary litany based on one from the organization Pax Christi. It shows Mary's continuing solidarity with the vulnerable and scorned in our world today. After each invocation, we repeat, first: Pray for us; and then: Lead us to life.

Pray:

Mary, our mother, *pray for us!*

Unwed mother . . .

Mother of the non-violent . . .

Mother of the political prisoner . . .

Mother of the condemned . . .

Mother of the dying . . .

Mother of the executed criminal . . .

Mother of the liberator . . .

Woman oppressed by religion, lead us to life.

Woman pregnant with hope . . .

Homeless woman . . .

Woman at the First Supper . . .

Political refugee . . .

Seeker of sanctuary . . .

Marginalized woman . . .

Woman of vision . . .

First disciple . . .

Comforter of the afflicted . . .

Woman always on mission . . .

Queen of peace . . .

Community Sharing: In this chapter, what attracted you? What puzzled you? What affirmed your experience? What challenged or stretched it? What helped you to love Mary more?

Chapter Eight

Growing in Wisdom and Grace:
Mary and Jesus

Returning to a theme from our first chapter, much of what we learn about Jesus in the New Testament is also true of Mary. We return to those five statements, in summary.

Hebrews states and Catholic tradition teaches that both he and she are like us in all things, but without sin. But what do we mean by sin? A careful reading of the gospels will show that Jesus was crucified, in part, because he overturned not just tables in the Temple, but also the very understanding of sin. Jesus understood sin as a weakening or breaking of relationship with God and/or with each other, not merely the breaking of a law. In the eyes of many of his contemporaries, he frequently broke the Law. Mary is without serious sin, we can be sure—serious sin as the Jews taught it. Such sin for them meant rebellion against God with a high hand (think of murder, idolatry, cheating the poor, abuse of power). Instead of rebellion, Mary cooperated with God's request in the beginning and throughout her life.

Jews also understood sin as "missing the mark." In our weakness we all fall short of our aim. Jesus himself was impatient with his disciples, disgusted with his enemies, called Peter a "Satan." In the same way, Mary would have had arguments with Joseph, or punished young Jesus at times, just as every human parent would. Jesus and Mary were both fully human. They would both have missed the mark. They were imperfect, and in that humanness, they were growing in wisdom and grace.

Jesus grew in wisdom, age, and grace, as Luke points out twice. So would Mary have grown. One grows in wisdom by experiencing and then by pondering the experience in the heart. A number of times, Luke explicitly offers this Marian way to grow in wisdom. Undoubtedly some of those experiences she pondered were mistakes to be corrected.

Reflect: How have you grown in wisdom? What part does reflection on your feelings, attitudes, and behavior play in your growth? What part do mistakes play? Ask for the grace to stay open to new experiences even as you age, and for the grace to learn from each experience just where Christ is at work in them.

Jesus and Mary were full of grace all their lives. When Gabriel called Mary full of grace, she was as full of grace as a pre-teen could be. How much greater her capacity for the life of God within her as she experienced daily dying and rising; fell more deeply in love with God, with Jesus, and with Joseph; loved and cared for the rest of her family and townspeople.

Mary, like Jesus, was a suffering servant: obedient, poor in spirit, chaste. Her obedience in Luke's annunciation scene has sometimes been used to keep women in a submissive role. Hers was a real choice, however; one that God respected. She, after questioning the messenger of God, was decisive in her cooperation, an adult kind of obedience. She was poor materially (although some scholars maintain that a craftsman's family led a middle class life), and poor in spirit, dependent on God for all that she learned and needed. She was chaste. Even if she and Joseph engaged in married sexual relations, they were chaste. Chastity is a gift God gives to all, no matter our state of life. It means reverence for the body and the boundaries of those whom we love. (Celibacy is the state of never being married, so Mary was not celibate.)

As Jesus preached good news and healed the sick, so did Mary. Perhaps she did so in a quite literal way in her mission after pentecost. As a member of the communion of saints, she continues her healing mission. We have ample evidence through twenty centuries that many have come to trust God through trusting her as mother, that many have been cured of disease through trusting Mary. Her shrines around the world are decorated with discarded bandages and crutches.

Jesus died to gather into one new family all the scattered children of God (Jn 11:52). Unity of all with all in God, *"you in me and I in you,"* was, and is, Christ's passionate desire. The Spirit is the bond of unity, and Mary continues to bear the Spirit, continues to gather into one new family all God's children scattered across the centuries and around the world.

As Jesus, so Mary, and now, so us. While those who have gone before us in faith undoubtedly share in God's perfect knowing and loving, and pray for us, so we too are anointed in baptism to grow in wisdom and grace. As members of the communion of saints ourselves, we are called to be obedient and coopera-tive with God, to be poor in spirit and chaste in body. We receive gifts for mission and ministry, and work to make tangible Jesus' passionate desire for our unity. Let us pray for Mary's support.

Pray:

Woman of good counsel and compassion . . . help us to ponder in our hearts.

Woman growing in wisdom and grace . . . share yours with us.

Woman like us in all things . . . help us to accept being human.

Sharer in Jesus' passion . . . help us not to numb our pain.

Witness of Christ's Resurrection . . . help us to find him alive in all things.

Woman fired by the Spirit . . . share your zeal with us.

Woman gifted for ministry . . . awaken us to our own gifts.

Woman powerful in mission . . . share your passion for the good news.

Woman of grace and truth, mercy and faithfulness . . . help us to embody Christ.

Woman centered in God . . . make us one in God, in Christ, in the Spirit. Amen.

Mary is our pioneer. While many generations have called her mother, and so many orphaned today on the killing fields of the world need her as mother, she is better situated as one of us, our sister or companion among the communion of saints. As Jesus himself is our pioneer through death into life (Heb 2:10; 12:2), so Mary has pioneered, blazed a trail for women. Like Jesus, she would have experienced all that we do, as we do, even the hormonal changes of pregnancy and menopause. When some protest that Jesus didn't have to endure the pain and neglect of old age, perhaps Mary pioneers for us just that experience.

Growing in wisdom, age, and grace is a lifelong process of being and becoming more deeply united with God in Christ. This calls for our cooperation; our willingness leads to our holiness as persons and as communities of faith. This is what Mary embodies, the holiness which springs from obedience to God's self-communication, and her cooperation with God's Spirit.

The Church community is *semper reformanda*, always reforming, according to Blessed Pope John XXIII. We have already begun to reform our understanding and appreciation of Jesus, Mary, and all that it means to be human. The Incarnation is not a split second in Mary's womb, but a lifelong process of Jesus' becoming fully human, fully alive. The Incarnation is mystery. Once we may not have dared to voice our questions in the face of mystery. Now, Karl Rahner, S.J., a premier Roman Catholic theologian of the last century, has assured us that what we call mystery is infinitely knowable. We will keep knowing more and more deeply for all eternity.

We are not to shut down our minds before what we cannot understand, but must keep on exploring, questioning, pondering, imagining. We will always be learning, knowing, revising, re-forming our understandings of Jesus, Mary, the Incarnation, and God's desire to give all to us in Jesus. God's further desire for us can be found in this prayer embedded in each eucharistic celebration. As the priest mixes a drop or two of water into the chalice of wine, he prays and let us pray too:

Pray: By the mingling of this water and wine, may we come to share in the divinity of Christ, who humbled himself to share in our humanity.

God's desire is that we might share the divinity of Christ. We are in the process of becoming more and more divine. The way to become more divine, paradoxically, is to become more human.

Community Sharing: In this chapter, what attracted you? What puzzled you? What affirmed your experience? What challenged or stretched it? What helped you love Jesus and Mary more?

Chapter Nine

In the Spirit:
Becoming Fully Human and Fully Alive

Throughout this work, we have continually emphasized the relationship of Mary and her son. We cannot finish it without specific mention of the relationship between Mary and the Holy Spirit. Across the centuries, when the experience of the Spirit would diminish in the faith life of the Christian community, devotion to Mary often filled the gap. In fact, many of the functions which Roman Catholics have assigned to Mary through the ages could be seen more appropriately as the movements of the Holy Spirit. The Spirit is our mothering creator, hovering over the abyss at the creation of the world, hovering over our own personal chaos. The Spirit is both the one who gifts and the gift, the love of God poured into our hearts. The Spirit is the seat of wisdom, our advocate, our counselor, our comforter, our defender. The Spirit is the one who links our spirit and God (Rom 8:26). Instead of Mary in the children's poem: "Lovely Lady dressed in blue, teach me how to pray . . ." it is the Spirit who teaches us to pray and who prays continually within us (Rom 8:26).

Twice in the scriptural narratives, Mary and the Spirit are intimately linked. First, the Spirit overshadows her to initiate the process of the Incarnation in her body (Lk 1:38). Later in her life, the Spirit fills her completely with missionary energy in the experience of pentecost (Acts 1:14). Like all of us, she is in the continual process of being made holy, sanctified in life and in death, by the power of the Spirit.

Obviously Mary is not co-equal with the Spirit, nor a kind of fourth member of the Holy Trinity. Pope John XXIII reminded us that Mary is not pleased when she is put above her Son. We might add, nor when she substitutes for the Holy Spirit. Mary is one of us in the Church, pioneer indeed, and surely our companion in the communion of saints, "truly our sister."

According to Elizabeth Johnson, Mary is so much more than a symbol. Johnson believes that while Mary may be the first of Jesus' disciples (meaning "learner"), she was not *the* iconic disciple. Other New Testament women such as Phoebe, Prisca, Junia, Joanna, and especially Martha and Mary of Bethany, were also devoted disciples. Mary of Magdala not only learned from Jesus but is named "apostle to the apostles," sent by Jesus to the men to announce that Jesus was raised from death. Johnson emphasizes:

First and foremost Mary is not a model, a type, an archetype, a prototype, an icon, a representative figure, a theological idea, an ideological cipher, a metaphor, a utopian principle, a feminine principle…an ideal [anyone]. . . . she is first and foremost herself. (Truly Our Sister, 100–01)

To be oneself. What gives God glory is to be our selves. As the early Church theologian St. Irenaeus taught, God's glory is the human being, fully human and fully alive. Like all of us, Mary was engaged in that paradoxical process of becoming more fully human so that she could become more fully divine. She was giving God glory in the smallest human task, the most ordinary prayer, the most humble gesture of love. She was authentic. And she kept on learning. She was entering day by day more deeply into the mystery of the Incarnation, that wonder-filled mix of human and divine. She was gradually penetrating mystery, that which is infinitely knowable. She was becoming more and more fully human.

As a human being, Mary was gifted with senses, intellect, will, memory, imagination, common sense, and the whole range of human feelings. In order to grow "com-passionate," to have passion with others, she needed to feel and accept her own deep feelings. As it was said of Jesus, "He had to become like us in every way so that he might be a compassionate and faithful high *priest"* (Heb 2:16), so Mary had to be like us every way. We ask her about her passions, her deep and long-lasting emotions, as Thomas Aquinas describes them. After asking her about each deep feeling listed below, listen for her response. It may be that some of these passions will speak more directly to your own experience. Stay with those which touch your own depths.

Pray: Mary, when were you ever lonely? afraid? hopeless? tender? sad? grateful?

Mary, when did you feel guilty? overjoyed? empty? jealous?

Mary, when did get furious? feel sexual?

Mary, when did you feel depressed? anxious? panic-stricken?

Mary, how did you handle conflict? When did your heart melt with love?

What did you hear from Mary, learn from Mary? Which emotions still trouble you? All these passions are God's gifts to us, neither right nor wrong. For example, anger is not a sin but a feeling. What we do with the feeling, how we behave, could be sinful or could be a sharing in God's passion for justice. Ask

Mary's guidance in appropriately expressing what you feel.

Like all of us, flesh and bones, Mary was a graced child, learning to walk, talk, relate with her parents and with other children. She laughed, cried, played, explored her neighborhood, was frightened, angry, wondered, and learned.

She, like all of us, learned. As a new adult in Jewish eyes, she learned that she was to be the mother of the one who would set us free from the ravages of sin, who would put flesh on the tender mercy and faithfulness of God. She learned what pregnancy meant to her body, to her emotional life, and to her spiritual life. She learned how to be a wife, to relate with a particular man, to love him and to let him love her. She learned how to travel, first to Elizabeth and then to Bethlehem. She learned the meaning of the labor of birthing, its pushing, its pain, and she was undoubtedly as trembling, anxious, and hopeful as any woman birthing a firstborn child. She had to learn how to be a mother to an infant, to a toddler with his stubborn ways, to a little boy who would come to her with his hungers and scraped knee and bruised ego. While there is little evidence that she left home to travel with Jesus to hear him preach, she was a lifelong learner of God and all the wondrous self-expressions of God in her world.

She, like all of us, loved. First, like all of us, she loved her parents, followed them, imitated them, and learned from them how to love, help, play, sing, and pray. She prayed psalms in her home. Women and girls did not have to attend the synagogue, but what teachings and songs might her father have brought into their house? For the Jews, to study scripture is to worship. Since boys learned to read by using the scrolls of Jewish scripture, and since the rabbis taught "Better for the scrolls of the Torah to fall into the fire than into the hands of a woman," she probably did not read. If not, she would be worshipping as she listened to the stories of her people interacting with their and her God. She began to "ponder" the events of her life in her heart. She meditated. She also "treasured" God at work in these events. She savored the God whom she found in all things. She contemplated. She knew how to look for God, and, as all good Jews did, to listen for God. She heard a word from an angel, according to Luke, and she learned the Word in her own womb. Or, according to Matthew, she heard the word of Joseph—to come to him, to go to Bethlehem, to go into hiding in Egypt, to find a home in Nazareth—and recognized in this man whom she loved the word of God for her and her baby.

She, like most of us, set up a home. In Luke 15:8–10, Jesus likens God to a housewife in search of a lost coin. As any little child would, how young Jesus must have watched his mother at home in Nazareth sweeping the dirt floor. She would have tended their little garden, fetched water from the common well and perhaps daily bread from the village oven. She would have baked and stirred and seasoned and ladled and washed up. She would have woven and washed the clothes, helped in the village fields at planting time and at harvest, and prepared the special meals that marked the liturgical feasts. She would have lit the candles to welcome the sabbath. And more. She would have opened her home to welcome the stranger and the stricken, and gone out to comfort the sick or the bereaved in the town.

Suddenly, she was the bereaved. Joseph died, Jesus left home. She had loved them so well, looking on with deep affection as the two would go off to work or to the synagogue. How proud she would have been as Jesus would practice reciting and singing the Torah in preparation for his bar mitzvah. Many years later, after a desert retreat, he returned to the synagogue in Nazareth *"in the power of the Spirit"* (Lk 4:14). The townspeople whom Mary had loved, worked with on common projects, and served in their need now *"wondered at the gracious words which proceeded from his mouth and asked, 'Is this not Joseph's son?'"* (Lk 4:22). However, as Jesus continued to preach that day, he emphasized the good news that all, even Gentiles, are included in God's love. Suddenly, "they were filled with wrath, rose up, put him out of the city and led him to the brow of the hill . . ." (Lk 4:29–30).

Contemplate, Dialogue: Imagine how Mary was feeling, what she was thinking, during this incident. These are her relatives and friends. This is her Jesus. Listen to her. Speak to her. Ask for the gift of offering compassion to Mary

What is the truth in this pericope that will nurture our life in abundance, our healing and freedom? Like us, Mary can feel betrayed, horrified, discouraged, angry, heartsick, the deepest grief as her townsfolk turn on her son. She loves, and to the extent of her love, so is her hurt that deep. How easy to love her parents, Joseph, and Elizabeth. Because she is learning always to love like Jesus (like God), however, in a universal, all-encompassing way, she has to learn to accept those who are different, even the enemy, and gradually to forgive—to let God "turn her tears into dancing." Forgiveness is not an act of her will. God grants her the gift of forgiveness and she can laugh again, making sure that there is plenty of wine for her neighbors and her friends in Cana. After Calvary, like us, she struggles to take in Jesus' words: "Father, forgive them," and to make them her own. She forgives Judas who betrayed him, the disciples who abandoned him, the Jewish and Roman authorities who killed him. Gradually. Does she need to forgive Jesus?

Like us, she is filled in a deeper, more mature way with the power of the Spirit at pentecost. As she ages, she is becoming even more fully human, more fully alive. She is sent to bring the good news, surely through her prayer and most likely in person. She is sent on mission, and she is gifted for ministry.

Ministry simply means service. Where did Jesus learn to wash feet, but from his mother? Where did he learn to overturn the values of this world about service, authority, and obedience? Where did he learn that women are valued partners in dialogue (cf. the Samaritan woman, Jn 4; and Martha, Jn 11), to be trusted with his self-revelations?

Reflect, Dialogue: And you, as you come to the end of this book? What has the Spirit revealed to you about Mary? How do you feel about Mary? Ask her to show you who she is and how she is, and how the two of you can grow ever closer.

Any human person—Mary and we ourselves—is a mystery. Hopefully, we know and will keep on knowing Mary now and all through eternity as a woman of flesh and bone, of passion and compassion. She still longs for, prays for, and helps effect peace and unity in the Christian churches and in the world.

Mary is a real person in her own right. We need not model our spiritual lives on hers, we need not even turn to her, pray to her, love her. However, as we try to be faithful to the Spirit's movements in our own hearts, we will most likely find that as our love of Jesus deepens and broadens, an awareness of Mary, mother of this One whom we love, will seep into our consciousness. Being with Mary will encourage our willing but adult obedience. She will travel with us on the journey as we become fully human, fully alive, and so give glory to God. She who was the first disciple of Jesus, learning the word of God and enfleshing the Word in her very body, is our friend and companion. Mary walks with us, prays with us, prepares us to meet the One whom she loves. With John the Baptizer, she might well say: *"He must increase, I must decrease."*

We conclude with this Celtic hymn, which reasserts and makes perfectly clear how the mother of the One whom we love leads us not to herself but to the One whom she loves, and whom now we all adore.

Mary the dawn, Christ the perfect day.

Mary the gate, Christ the heavenly way.

Mary the root, Christ the mystic vine.

Mary the grape, Christ the sacred wine.

Mary the wheat-sheaf, Christ the living bread.

Mary the rose tree, Christ the rose blood-red.

Mary the fount, Christ the cleansing flood.

Mary the chalice, Christ the saving blood.

Mary the beacon, Christ the haven's rest.

Mary the mirror, Christ the vision blest.

Communal Prayer: Thank you, Mary, for opening your heart to us, for loving us so well. Thank you for your inclusive love, for your accepting us just as we are. Thank you for giving us Jesus once in the flesh, and always now through the Spirit. Thank you that at the cross, you stood, as helpless as we, the body of Christ, are in the face of our suffering world. Thank you for the power exhibited in your mission and ministry then, and now. In joy, in sorrow, in birth, in death, in all the daily-ness, you are like us in all things, fully human, fully alive, giving God the glory. Thank you!

Community Sharing: In this chapter, what attracted you? What puzzled you? What affirmed your experience? What challenged or stretched it? What in this chapter helped you to love Mary more?

For Further Reading

Borg, Marcus, and NT Wright. *The Meaning of Jesus*. HarperSanFrancisco, 1999.

Brown, Raymond. *An Adult Christ at Christmas*. Collegeville, MN: Liturgical Press, 1978.

Brown, Raymond, Karl Donfried et al., eds. *Mary in the New Testament*. Philadelphia: Fortress Press, 1978.

Cunneen, Sally. *In Search of Mary*. New York: Ballentine Books, 1996.

Donnelly, Doris, ed. *Mary: Woman of Nazareth*. Mahwah, NJ: Paulist Press, 1989.

Hazeleton, Lesley. *Mary*. New York: Bloomsbury, 2004.

Johnson, Elizabeth, C.S.J. *Friends of God and Prophets*. New York: Continuum, 1998.

———. *Truly Our Sister: A Theology of Mary in the Communion of Saints*. New York: Continuum, 2003.

Maloney, Robert, C.M. "The Historical Mary," *America*, vol. 193, #20, December 19, 2005, pp. 12–15.

The Mary Puge: www.udayton.edu/mary

Pelikan, Jaroslav. *Mary Through the Centuries: Her Place in the History of Culture*. New Haven: Yale University Press, 1996.

Tambasco, Anthony. *What Are They Saying about Mary?* Mahwah, NJ: Paulist Press, 1984.

Rea McDonnell, S.S.N.D., holds a PhD in Biblical Studies. She trained as a pastoral counselor at the Institute for Pastoral Psychology and for the past thirty-five years has used a pastoral approach to scripture in preparing adults for priestly and lay ministry. In addition to working as an adjunct faculty member and leading workshops and retreats, she has authored or coauthored thirteen books. She currently resides in Maryland where she ministers as a spiritual director.

More on Ignatian Spirituality

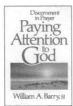